Gerald Norris is an acknowledged expert on the maritime history of th… its pirates and buccane… *Voyages* for the Folio S… in Devon. He is marriec…

Frontispiece
Blackbeard, an engraving from
Daniel Defoe's *The King of Pirates* (1724)

West Country Pirates and Buccaneers

GERALD NORRIS

DOVECOTE PRESS

for
my Sally

First published in 1990 by The Dovecote Press Ltd
Stanbridge, Wimborne, Dorset BH21 4JD

ISBN 0 946159 86 6

Photoset in Palatino by The Typesetting Bureau Ltd
Wimborne, Dorset
Printed and bound by Biddles Ltd,
Guildford and King's Lynn

Contents

Introduction

GEOGRAPHICAL position and the natural advantages afforded by its coastline made the West Country a seafaring community. As a result, Dorset, Somerset, Devon and Cornwall produced many of England's most celebrated mariners: Drake, Hawkins, Raleigh, Blake, Hood and great explorers like Humphrey Gilbert, John Davis and George Somers. But not all those 'that go down to the sea in ships, that do business in great waters', possess worthy aims, and the region has given birth to an equal number of nautical villains.

You will find in the following pages tales of a score or so of the West Country's most memorable pirates. They were not necessarily the most successful. William Parker of Plymouth and John Hawley of Dartmouth had such prosperous careers that they rose to become mayors of their towns; if their undoubtedly notable deeds had been more colourful, they would have received space here. It would have been pleasant also to include John Chudleigh, a twenty-four-year-old Devon squire who sold all his estates to finance a freebooting voyage to Peru; but he never did any pirating, since he, his crew and ship were lost after only a dozen days at sea. Another pirate who deserves mention is Thomas Fleming. It was he who first sighted the Armada and by rushing the news back to Plymouth voluntarily delivered himself into the hands of the authorities – who later granted him a pardon.

For those who want to know the differences between various sorts of pirates, here are some definitions.

Pirate. Somebody who commits robbery on the seas, also called a rover or freebooter.

Privateer. Somebody furnished with a letter of marque or other official licence commissioning him to attack and rob enemy merchant shipping.

Buccaneer. A pirate who preyed almost exclusively on Spanish vessels in the Caribbean around the second half of the seventeenth century, also called a filibuster. The pretence existed that the buccaneers were actually privateers, though they seldom held official commissions. The word *buccaneer* comes from the French *boucanier*, describing somebody who barbecues meat. The buccaneers were originally French, Dutch and English hunters of wild cattle in the West Indies before they found it more lucrative to rob the Spanish.

Corsair. Usually a foreign pirate or privateer – a word capable of wide interpretation.

In *Prejudice and Promise in Fifteenth Century England* (1962) C. L. Kingsford has written, 'To his enemies Francis Drake, though the greatest of Elizabethan seamen, was but an arch-pirate, and his earliest exploits were of a character which could not be justified on any modern principle of naval warfare. But whether as pirate or patriot, he was the successor of a long line of west country seamen, who by their achievements, legitimate or otherwise, helped to lay the foundations of English maritime supremacy.' If the Battle of Waterloo was won on the playing fields of Eton, then perhaps the Battle of Trafalgar was won on the pirate sloops and smuggling smacks of the West Country.

GERALD NORRIS

1

Blackbeard · Demon King of the Pirates

Have you heard of Teach the rover,
And his knavery on the Main,
How of gold he was a lover,
How he loved ill-gotten gain?

BLACKBEARD's real name was Edward Teach, or perhaps Thatch, and he came from Bristol. He has gone down in history as the most terrifying of all pirates, which seems to have been his intent, for he took pains to cultivate an appearance to match his reputation.

Blessed by nature with a towering physique and vast quantities of hair, he also had a twisted nose and cauliflower ears. In *A General History of the Robberies and Murders of the Most Notorious Pyrates* (1724) Daniel Defoe says that his whiskers, 'like a frightful Meteor, covered his whole face, and frightened America more than any Comet.'

> This Beard was black, which he suffered to grow of an extravagant Length; as to Breadth, it came up to his Eyes; he was accustomed to twist it with Ribbons, in small Tails, after the Manner of our Ramilies Wiggs, and turn them about his Ears. In Time of Action, he wore a Sling over his Shoulders, with three Brace of Pistols, hanging in Holsters, like Bandaliers; and stuck lighted Matches under his Hat, which appearing on each Side of his Face, his Eyes naturally looking fierce and wild, made him altogether such a Figure, that Imagination cannot form an Idea of a Fury, from Hell, to look more frightful.

These matches were not today's little sticks but lengths of fuse cord impregnated with saltpetre and limewater; six inches lasted half an hour, glowing, reeking, fizzing, and wreathing his head in smoke.

Ever mindful of his image, he deliberately devised situations in which to reinforce his reputation. Once he dared the toughest members of his crew, 'Let us make a hell of our own and try how long we can bear it'. Three men accepted the challenge and followed him into the hold, shutting all the hatches. He ordered them to set alight pots of brimstone, and all four seated themselves in a circle as the air slowly turned yellow with sulphurous fumes. One by one the crewmen rose from their stools, staggered to the hatches and clambered up on deck. Some minutes later Blackbeard appeared, queasy but triumphant. On another occasion, amid heavy drinking, he suddenly drew out a pair of pistols beneath the table, extinguished the candle and cocked them in an uneasy silence. After a lengthy pause, he discharged both weapons, shooting a man through the knee, laming him for life. He did this, he explained, so people should not forget who he was.

During the two years of his colourful career he is supposed to have married more than a dozen girls, many of them no more than fifteen years old. He particularly enjoyed watching them have intercourse with other men. Such was his appetite that he sometimes invited as many as six messmates to present to them in succession.

His piratical deeds are less diverting and amount to little more than a short record of solid, if unremarkable, achievement.

He came to public attention in 1716, moving from the Bahamas to the Carolinas and Virginia. He found an ally in the Governor of North Carolina, Charles Eden, who, for a consideration, held a court of Vice-Admiralty and ruled him to be not a pirate but a privateer in service of the Crown. This effectively gave him *carte blanche* to waylay any ship that took his fancy, and he roamed Pamlico Sound and Raleigh Bay without check. It is interesting to note that, despite his reputation, there is no record of his misusing passengers or crew of any captured vessels. His downfall came from interrupting Virginian shipping. In November 1718 prominent North Carolina businessmen, knowing of Governor Eden's corruption, sent a delegation to Governor Alexander Spotswood of Virginia asking him to put an end to Blackbeard's activities. Spotswood, who had fought with Marlborough at Blenheim, was delighted to be given this pretext for exceeding his authority and presently dispatched into Raleigh Bay two fully manned sloops under the command of Lieutenant Robert Maynard.

The pirate had anchored in shallow and treacherous water between two islands dividing Raleigh Bay from Pamlico Sound. This narrow channel, Ocracoke Inlet, has a depth of no more than ten feet and even today is navigated only by local fishermen. Maynard tracked him there by November 22nd, then suffered the calamity of having both sloops go aground on an ebbing tide. Blackbeard could now make for the open sea, yet decided first to teach his pursuers a lesson and opened fire with grape and chain shot, splintering the mainmast of one of the sloops, cutting away her sails and rigging, and killing nine crew. This proved a miscalculation; the tide was running fast, and he paid the penalty by grounding. Meanwhile, the undamaged sloop, commanded by Maynard, had been freed from the sand bar. When Blackbeard saw her approaching, he downed a great bowl of rum, bellowed damnation to all and sundry, stuffed several more pistols in his belt and ordered another broadside, devastating the sloop and removing a further twenty-one men from the fray. This attack was followed by a torrent of homemade grenades filled with small shot and scrap iron. Nevertheless, the sloop came on, and the two vessels slammed together.

The massive shaggy-bearded pirate vaulted on to the enemy deck, gun blazing, cutlass flaying, his crew swelling behind him. Swiftly identifying Maynard as leader of the Virginians, he scythed and blasted a path towards him until only bare boards lay between them. He pulled a pistol from his sling and fired, and Maynard fired too. Incredibly, Blackbeard's shot missed, but the lieutenant's lodged in his

Blackbeard's last fight.

adversary's chest. However, the pirate came lumbering on as if nothing had happened. Maynard kept his nerve and, timing the blow perfectly, drove his sword forward with tremendous power. But Blackbeard, displaying the most amazing reflexes, swept his cutlass across the thrust and snapped the sword off at the hilt, leaving the lieutenant defenceless. And so their duel drew to its close; the cutlass was raised to deliver the final blow. Yet, even as it fell, a Virginian sword sliced into the pirate's throat, for one of Maynard's seamen had leapt to his rescue. The lieutenant dodged the faltering blade, cocked his pistol and fired point-blank. Blackbeard fought on, spouting blood and roaring obscenities. It took another four shots and half-dozen sword slashes before he toppled to the deck lifeless.

Only nine of his men were left, and they immediately surrendered. His head was cut off and hung from the bowsprit of the sloop. His body and those of the other dead pirates were dumped overboard 'till the Sea was tinctur'd with Blood round the Vessel.'

News reached Williamsburg before Maynard's return. When he sailed up the James river, people were already thronging the shore to catch a glimpse of the huge matted head swinging to and fro.

Blackbeard's head suspended from the bowsprit of Lieutenant Maynard's sloop, HMS Pearl.

2
THE BRIEF EXPLOITS OF CAPTAIN PHILLIPS

JOHN Phillips hailed from Lympstone, two miles north of Exmouth. In 1723 he went to Newfoundland, where he worked in a cod fishery at Saint-Pierre. He soon tired of such employment and on the night of August 29th, together with four other young men, stole a Boston schooner anchored in the harbour.

Once out to sea, they drew up articles of association, mostly with regard to sharing of booty, shipboard discipline and preparation for engagements. Two of these articles are of special interest, since they relate to compensation and chivalry, subjects that may not have concerned more weatherbeaten rovers:

8. If any Man shall lose a Joint in Time of an Engagement, he shall have 400 Pieces of Eight; if a Limb 800.
9. If at any Time you meet with a prudent Woman, that Man that offers to meddle with her, without her Consent, shall suffer present Death.

They renamed the schooner *Revenge* and elected Phillips captain. Although so few in number, they caught several fishing vessels within their first week 'on the account.' However, being in a hurry to enlarge their crew, they not only persuaded seamen on captured ships to join them, but impressed many against their inclinations. Further prizes ensured that a proportion of these latter conscripts became reconciled to their new occupation, yet the dissidents also grew greater. Consumed by their own success and untutored in men or the ways of the world, Phillips and his four colleagues failed to recognize the forces that were gathering against them.

By February 1724 they had seized twenty vessels while cruising down to the West Indies and back up the Eastern Seaboard. During that month the *Revenge* intercepted a ship off the coast of New Jersey, and a crew was put aboard. But the men made away with her, and Phillips gave immediate pursuit. Soon drawing alongside, he ordered them back on the *Revenge*. When they refused, he shot one man dead, hitting another in the leg. The rest then surrendered, and the injured man had his leg sawn off by the carpenter. After a further prize was taken, some rebels attempted a second escape, but Phillips again caught up with them and killed two more.

Now steeped in blood, his character became baser, his manner increasingly malevolent. The captain of the next captured ship found him so insufferable that he snatched up a capstan bar and struck him over the head. Phillips must have been singularly strong, for he endured this without flinching before running the man through with his sword.

Continuing up the Atlantic Coast, the pirates wrested another ten prizes during March and early April. In seven months their haul amounted to thirty-three; apart from the fishing vessels, they had appropriated three brigantines, four schooners and four sloops. On April 14th the *Revenge* was skirting the Isles of Shoals off the coast of New Hampshire when she fell in with a trim new sloop, the *Squirrel*, out of Annisquam, near Gloucester, Massachusetts. Phillips fired a shot across her bows and hoisted a black flag emblazoned with a white skeleton. Captain Haraden of the *Squirrel* anxious to avoid damage to his fine vessel, instantly hove to, had himself rowed to the *Revenge* and surrendered. To his dismay, he was told the marauders were abandoning their ship and commandeering his, which would be converted into a full-scale frigate mounting more than two dozen guns. As soon as the ordnance had been transferred, most of his men were put aboard the *Revenge* to fend for themselves, while he and a few others were impressed as pirates for the *Squirrel*.

Captain Haraden thus found himself a deckhand on his own ship, with the sound of hammer, saw and splintering wood ringing in his ears as crude alterations were hastily made. He sought out the leading dissenters, and a new determination was forged below the hatches.

Three days later the right moment suddenly presented itself, a signal was given, and the ship's master and boatswain were attacked simultaneously. According to Daniel Defoe in his *Pyrates*, one of the conspirators, the carpenter Edward Cheeseman,

'seizes Nutt (master) by the Collar, and putting one Hand between his Legs, toss'd him over the side of the Vessel, but, he holding by Cheeseman's

Sleeve, said, *Lord have Mercy upon me! what are you going to do, Carpenter?* He told him it was an unnecessary Question, for, says he, *Master, you are a dead Man*, so strikes him over the Arm, Nutt loses his Hold, tumbles into the Sea, and never spoke more. By this time the Boatswain was dead; for as soon as Philmore [greatgrandfather of President Millard Fillmore] saw the Master laid hold of, he raised up the Ax, and divided his Enemy's head in two.'

The commotion produced by eliminating the captain's two chief partners brought Phillips himself bounding up on deck, whose arrival Cheeseman 'saluted with a Blow of a Mallet, which broke his Jaw-Bone, but did not knock him down.' Phillips continued to display uncommon durability until Captain Haraden hit him over the head with a heavy steel adze, crushing his skull.

Captain Haraden took command of the *Squirrel* again and sailed her back to Annisquam. In imitation of Lieutenant Maynard's return to Virginia, Phillips's head was cut off and hung from the bowsprit. Later, when required at the Massachusetts Court of Admiralty, it was sent to Boston in a pickle barrel.

The only surviving member of the original five, William White, aged twenty-two, was sentenced to death together with an early recruit, John Rose Archer, twenty-seven, who had once sailed with Blackbeard. The famous clergyman Cotton Mather preached a sermon to them on Sunday May 31st 1724, and two days afterwards they were hanged at the Charlestown Ferry in Boston. Archer's body was suspended in iron bands and chains for many weeks on Bird Island – which stood between Governors Island and Noddle's Island and was later washed away.

3
The Pirates of Lundy Island

1 WILLIAM DE MARISCO

LUNDY Island, eleven miles off Hartland Point, commands the entrance to the Bristol Channel. Remoteness and inaccessability made it an ideal stronghold for pirates, who used it from earliest times. The best known family to live there were the Mariscos, who held the island for two centuries. They also owned lands in Somerset, at Cameley and Huntspill, and on a more extensive scale in Ireland, where their political manoeuvres caused Henry III such irritation that he threw several of them into prison and confiscated three of their properties.

When Geoffrey de Marisco and his son William were eventually released from Kilkenny Castle at the end of 1234, their most bitter grievance was in each having also now to pay a huge fine of £2,000. Since they maintained they had never been disloyal to the King, they petitioned him to reconsider, but to no avail. Early in May 1235 they travelled to London in an effort to vindicate themselves and have their penalties squashed. However, they reckoned without the simultaneous arrival at court of Henry Clement, the wily and eloquent emissary of the Justiciar of Ireland. Clement, an avowed enemy, presented himself at the proceedings and, tormenting them with subtle insinuations, began to undermine the King's newfound inclination towards forgiveness.

Clement was lodging in Westminster with a surgeon, Master David, at his house opposite the main gate of the royal palace. Around one o'clock on the morning of Monday May 14th, more than a dozen horsemen clattered to a halt outside Master David's. Six of them jumped from their horses, raced to the front door and smashed it off its hinges. They bounded up the stairs, broke down another door and came face to face with Clement, who ran to the window and was about to jump when, spotting the men below, he turned back into the room and was stabbed to death.

There were quite a few witnesses, including servants of Master David and a handful of the King's guards from across the street. Too frightened or sleepy to do much, they recognized none of the assailants. An inquiry was held, at which Master David recollected that a boy in buttons, messenger of William de Marisco, had called more than once during the last week to ask whether Clement was still staying there; and Clement had confided to Master David that he felt his life was in danger because some of William's men had earlier made threats to him.

It was concluded that William de Marisco had been responsible for the murder, and this belief was strengthened by his headlong flight west, which ended not in Somerset or Ireland but on Lundy. He and his men were at once proclaimed outlaws, though nothing was done to bring them to justice, since the island was considered with justification virtually impenetrable. The rest of his lands in Ireland were now confiscated, leaving him with insufficient income on which adequately to survive. Left with no alternative, he turned pirate.

The day of the Spanish galleon and richly laden Dutch East Indiaman had not yet come, nor of the powerful frigate that could range the seas and catch them. William was forced to work hard for his living, picking up anything he encountered and being limited to domestic waters, from the Scillies to the Mull of Galloway and across as far as County Cork. He built up a fleet of galleys that preyed continuously on shipping in the Bristol Channel and Irish Sea. His men were ruthless, killing and wounding those who showed the slightest sign of resistance. Apart from robbing vessels, they abducted merchants and other prosperous travellers, imprisoning them on Lundy and demanding large sums for their release.

Despite his success, William was not content. Having been a prominent landowner, he resented being branded an outlaw and leading so restricted an existence. After three years on Lundy, he was consumed with such hatred for Henry III that he wanted him exterminated. Accordingly a knight was dispatched to the court at Woodstock, where his attempt at regicide had a circuitousness bordering on eccentricity.

Arriving in September 1238, he suavely infiltrated the palace courtiers and eventually moved into the King's presence. Catching his Majesty's eye, he addressed him thus: 'Resign to me the kingdom that you have unjustly usurped and long retained!', adding that he bore the mark of royalty on his shoulder. This was designed to establish his insanity and proved effective, for when the King's servants offered to beat him, Henry admonished them, saying 'Leave the madman alone, let him rave in his folly; the words of such people have not the force of truth.'

During the early hours of the following morning the knight climbed through the window of the King's sleeping chamber and crept over to his bed. Raising his knife, he noticed Henry was not in bed. He began looking for him in other parts of the chamber. He did this so conscientiously that one of the Queen's ladies-in-waiting, Margaret Bisset, who had been reciting her psalter by the light of a candle, became alarmed at the noise of his oaths as he stumbled about the room. She peeped in, saw him searching every corner and ran for help. The royal guards burst into the bedchamber and seized him. After being bound in chains and tortured, he confessed to coming at the behest of William de Marisco. He was taken to Coventry, roped to horses and ripped limb from limb.

Henry now issued directives to the Sheriffs of Somerset, Devon and other counties and to the Bailiffs of ports such as Minehead and Barnstaple that they must take more strenuous steps to capture William and destroy his operations. But Lundy, with its sheer cliffs and single harbour, remained impregnable, while William, according to the chronicles, grew stronger, 'having attached to himself many outlaws and malefactors, subsisting by piracies, taking more especially wine and provisions and making frequent sudden eruptions on the adjacent lands, spoiling and injuring the realm by land and by sea.'

In December 1241, three years after the Woodstock episode, the Sheriff of Devon at last succeeded in arresting some of William's men; they were taken to Winchester and there imprisoned. This encouraged Henry to try to dislodge William once and for all, and he instructed his Council to plan a raid on Lundy, using any men and equipment they required. A dashing Norfolk nobleman, William Bardolph, was chosen as leader of the expedition and given fifteen men, mostly from Devon and Bristol. They rowed across to Lundy, possibly from Bideford, on a suitably misty day towards the end of May 1242 and accurately brought their boats with muffled oars to the one spot where they stood a chance of scaling the cliff.

With skill and patience they inched their way up the almost perpendicular rockface, but a few yards short of the top were startled to discover an armed sentinel suddenly looming against the sky. By a stroke of good fortune, he turned out to be a man who had lost faith with William and remained on the island against his inclinations. Once Bardolph, in the advance group, had promised a pardon if he helped them, the man offered his support, assisted each climber to the top and led them through thick fern and heather to William's stronghold. The pirates were sitting eating, totally unprepared. Bardolph gathered his troops, sprang through the doorway and, leaping on William, pressed a dagger to his throat. The other pirates were also quickly overpowered, then trussed with stout cord.

They were bundled onto William's own vessels, taken to Bristol and held in the castle, the guard being strengthened with constables and burgesses. A few days later, they were transferred to London, where William was placed in the Tower and most of his men in either Newgate or the Fleet. William was tried at Westminster for treason and murder, found guilty and condemned to death. On Friday July 25th 1242 he was dragged by horse to the gibbet, his head bumping and bouncing over the cobbles. To the very last, he protested himself innocent of killing Henry Clement or attempting to assassinate the King; he had fled to Lundy simply to avoid Henry's anger; as a pirate, he had done no more than pilfer a few necessities to eke out his wretched existence.

William was hanged, then suspended on a hook and disembowelled. While his bowels were being burnt, his body was quartered. The quarters were sent for exhibition in other cities, one portion travelling as far as Oxford.

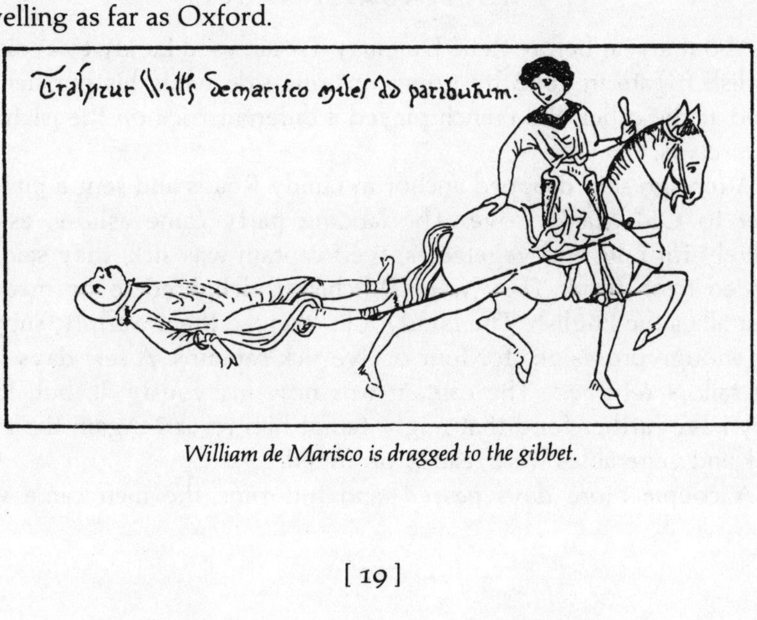

William de Marisco is dragged to the gibbet.

2 THOMAS SALKELD

Over the centuries many pirates followed William de Marisco's example and used Lundy as their base, often for only brief periods. In 1542 French marauders occupied the island until their ships were burnt by a flotilla of Covelly fishermen. During the 1620s and 30s it was the turn of Spaniards and Algerians, who carried away some of the inhabitants to sell as slaves.

Lundy's oddest pirate was undoubtedly Thomas Salkeld. He yearned for status and, having set foot on the island, declared himself its King. Official reports state that on March 23rd 1610 he 'went with his men and his colours and took the island of Lundy in defiance of the king of England and wished his Majesty's heart upon the point of his sword, and called himself king of Lundy.' He captured a few insignificant vessels, took a handful of prisoners, shaved their heads and called them his slaves. Having set up a gallows, he mustered the dozen or so islanders and slaves beneath it and compelled them to swear an oath of allegiance acknowledging his kingship while he pointed a cautionary finger at the alternative above.

George Eskott from Appledore, an officer on board a little merchant ship seized by Salkeld, eventually led a revolt of the slaves, thereby earning himself immortality as the Spartacus of Lundy Island. He and several others, having no weapons, threw some stones at Salkeld, who ran away and was not seen again.

3 HOLLENDAISE SAUCE

About a year before René Du Guay-Trouin used Lundy to avoid an English frigate in 1692 by going out one side while his pursuer entered at the other, the French played a different trick on the islanders themselves.

A foreign ship dropped anchor in Lundy Roads and sent a pinnace over to Old Man's Cove. The landing party came ashore, asking politely for milk and vegetables; their captain was sick, they said, he needed fresh food. They were Dutchmen, delighted to be meeting their allies the English. The Lundy folk received them warmly, supplying enough provisions for four or five sick captains. A few days later the sailors returned. The captain was now grievously ill, but could they have further food that might tempt him to eat? Again the fresh milk and vegetables were readily proffered.

A couple more days passed, and this time the men came with

downcast heads: the captain had died. His last wish was not to be buried at sea but among those whom he had looked on as his friends. Might they lay him to rest in some corner of the Lundy churchyard?

The coffin was brought ashore, across Tent Field and up Beacon Hill to St Anne's. The interior of the little chapel had been tastefully decorated with lilies and ferns. All the local people attended the service as a mark of respect. About halfway through, the leader of the crew asked if he and his colleagues could share some moments alone with the departed. The islanders discreetly withdrew and gathered outside the door, waiting to be recalled for the conclusion of the ceremony.

Not long afterwards the door was thrown open, and the mourners emerged, each man armed with musket and cutlass. Lundy's entire population stood wide-eyed and affrighted, quickly encircled by their former friends. They were brusquely herded back into the chapel, where a half-dozen of the crew mounted guard. Before the altar lay the empty coffin and, beside it, odds and ends of sacking in which the weapons had been wrapped.

The French corsairs – the pretence was over – now ransacked every house and store, removing anything of value and carrying it off to their ship, even sheep and goats. They made a clean sweep of Lundy and nailed fast the chapel door, which withstood the islanders long enough for the raiders to spread sail and clear Surf Point.

4
The First Pirate Hero

To countries such as France and Spain, 'Arripay' of Poole was an out-and-out pirate, like 'Francisco Drak' two centuries later. To the English, he was a great maritime hero and patriot. Even today certain works of reference, including the *Dictionary of National Biography,* call him simply a 'sea captain', which is turning a blind eye to most of his exploits. He would sometimes arrive back from a raid along the Breton coast with a dozen foreign ships in tow; he might equally well return with a prize picked off the shores of Kent or Sussex. The distinction between privateering and piracy appears to have either eluded him or never gained his interest.

Harry Pay is believed to have been born in about 1365 in the centre of Poole, in Dorset, near the corner of Carters Lane and Hill Street. He came to prominence in 1395 when he sacked and razed Gijón on the northwest coast of Spain and attacked Santa Maria de Finisterre, near Corunna, carrying off its priceless crucifix. This was the overture to numerous sorties in the Bay of Biscay; he inflicted severe damage on seaports around San Sebastián, seized ships and prisoners and exacted large ransoms. He also waylaid Spanish vessels in the Channel. His return home was always a red-letter day in the life of Poole, and we are told that 'puncheons of good Porto wine and kegs of brandy were broached, so that there was scarcely a sober man in town.'

His brigandage seems eventually to have gone too far. in 1402 he was arraigned before the Privy Council by demand of the King of Castile, who insisted that these forays contravened the prevailing truce between England and Castile. Harry succeeded in withstanding the charge, probably with help from important patrons. He undoubtedly enjoyed royal favour at the time, because in April 1401 he was given command of the flotilla conveying Henry IV's daughter

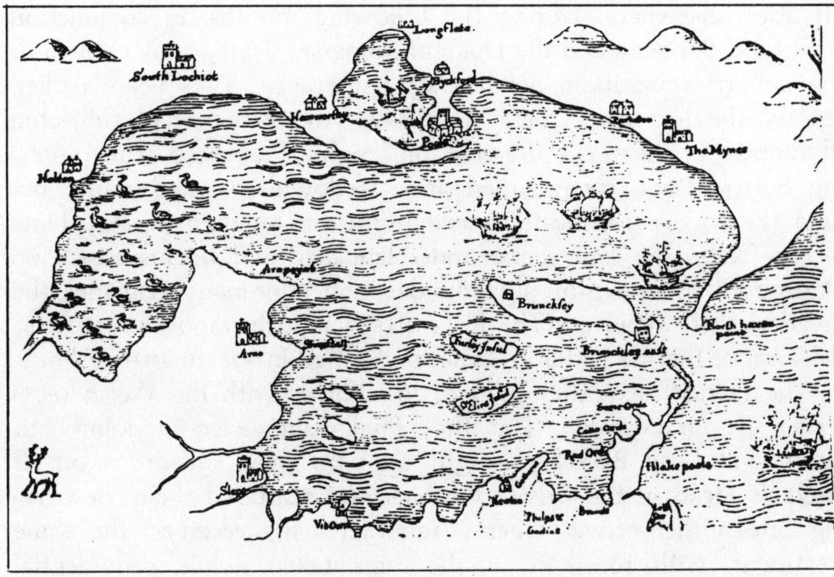

A view of Poole Harbour in the early 17th century. Poole itself can be seen on the north side (marked by the church), Brownsea Island sits between the two arms of the harbour entrance.

Blanche, and a dowry of 16,000 gold nobles, to Germany for her wedding to Louis Count Palatine of the Rhine.

Henry is unlikely to have approved of his next escapade, for he captured a richly laden German carrack sailing back from Spain. This was straightforward piracy and a tactless blow to the King's foreign diplomacy. Yet he somehow managed to continue unchecked and in 1403 took two Spanish caravels, one with a full cargo of wine, the other carrying 160 tons of Bilbao iron. In 1404 he was required to answer charges of piracy regarding a further Spanish merchantman that he robbed of gold, silver, various luxury goods and another 115 tons of iron. It was maintaianed that he killed some of the Castilian crew, setting others adrift in a cockleboat in mid-Channel. Although he was ordered to make restitution, there is no evidence to suggest he did. Instead, he forthwith took the *Santa Maria* of Bilbao, relieving her of iron, oil, wax, suet and hides worth £4,000.

We must surmise that Henry IV chose to pretend ignorance of Harry's misdemeanours, just as Elizabeth I did with Drake's: both men were too useful to cast aside. The King now directed the pirate's attention elsewhere. During the following months, in conjunction with Lord Berkeley and the Duke of Somerset, Harry took control of the country's maritime defence against France. Two years earlier, led by the legendary Sieur du Chätel, the French had subjected Plymouth to the most dreadful onslaught. Prevented from entering Sutton Pool, they landed at Cattedown, marched round behind the town's fortifications and burnt six hundred houses. Nine months later, the same commander launched a ferocious attack on Dartmouth, but was mortally wounded, and, after many casualties, the invaders were repulsed. The King attached such importance to this deliverance that he had a *Te Deum* performed in Westminster Abbey.

The French next attempted to join forces with the Welsh rebel leader Owain Glyndŵr. This they finally succeeded in doing, but Harry and Lord Berkeley caught up with their squadrons off St Govan's Head in the Bristol Channel and scattered them, destroying fifteen men-of-war. Enemy reinforcements received the same treatment, with fourteen supply ships taken, while providential storms also came to England's aid, scotching the development of other French manoeuvres. In retribution, Harry commanded an expedition that ravaged forty villages along the coasts of Brittany, Calvados and Picardy. He returned with one hundred and twenty captured vessels and booty of iron, oil, wine and salt.

Charles VI of France, who had fretted himself into madness, and Henry III of Castile, retrospectively known as 'the Sufferer', having each had enough of the English and Arripay, now planned a massive joint assault on West Country ports. An armada of more than forty ships was projected, to be equipped at Santander in Spain, but in the end the fleet amounted to only five caravels, with full complements of archers, arbalesters (the arbalest was a huge medieval crossbow) and foot soldiers. They were led by Charles de Savoisi, a childhood friend of Charles VI, and the rugged Spanish commander Don Pedro Niño. Their campaign began brightly in August 1405 with the sacking of Looe. Travelling east, they encountered sterner opposition and were repulsed off Plymouth and Portland. By now de Savoisi had become somewhat cautious, and when they reached Poole, he declined to attack it, even though one of the principal objectives of the expedition had been to root out the nest of pirates that had caused both countries such tribulation. Don Pedro, however, had lost none of his zest for a fight, and disembarked some of his troops. Despite the absence of Harry Pay, the people of Poole offered fierce resistance, driving their

Harry Pay commanded ships similar to this.

assailants back onto the quay. Don Pedro then threw in the rest of his forces, who soon proved impossible to check. From the security of their boats, the French bowmen added to the onslaught. Doors had to be ripped from their hinges and used as protection against the hefty arbalest bolts. But to no avail, for Don Pedro and his men finally looted the town and put much of it to the torch. Flames still leapt in the sky as their caravels quit the harbour on the voyage back to France. Several years passed before Poole regained its prosperity.

Harry had lost a brother and many of his friends. During the next months he remorselessly dealt out a series of stinging reprisals and, less mindful than usual of his own safety, suffered the indignity of being captured off the coast of Normandy. A French chronicler wrote, 'What conferred such distinction on this little triumph was that France's most implacable enemy, Harry Pay himself, was on board.' But the triumph was shortlived. While the English sailors knelt on the enemy deck in prayer, hearing each other's confession before execution, the French skipper imprudently took more than half his crew onto Harry's ship to search for booty. Harry waited for them to work their way down to the storerooms and hold, then gave a signal. His men sprang at the guards, overpowered them and grabbed their weapons. Jumping into the stern of the French vessel, they struck down those who still remained. They scrambled onto their own ship just in time to deal with the Frenchmen emerging from the hatches. In only a few minutes, they had won back the ship and clapped the French survivors in irons. In a victorious gesture, Harry sailed several miles up the Seine, defiantly flying the captured flag of Valois. That same year he brought into Poole more than a hundred barques taken in French waters.

These exploits proved to be the climax of his career, for we hear little more of him after this. He was approaching fifty, an almost venerable age for those days. He managed to waylay a ship belonging to a London merchant and relieve it of forty-nine tuns of beer, worth £294, but this inglorious act of piracy appears to have been his last. The death in 1413 of Henry IV, whom he had served so well, probably brought about his retirement. Henry V employed him on work for the Cinque Ports as an inspector of fortifications. He died on March 25th 1419 and was buried at Faversham, near Canterbury, in the Church of St Mary of Charity, where he is honoured with a memorial brass. His death came four years after the great victory of Agincourt heralded the dawn of England's rise to European power.

5
The Pirates of Studland

1 JOHN PIERS

DURING the second half of the sixteenth century Studland Bay, between Swanage and Poole, was among the most frequented pirate anchorages in Britain. The system of tides there gave ships a chance of putting to sea seventeen hours in every twenty-four, which meant they could often embark at a moment's notice. A number of wealthy Purbeck landowners helped finance the pirates, and local jurisdiction was claimed by several authorities, leading to confusion and corruption. As a result, many infamous West Country sea-rovers found their way to this remote stretch of Dorset coast.

John Piers came from Padstow in Cornwall and may have been born in about 1550. He is described as 'a tall sklender man havinge longe black heare on his hed hanginge almoast downe to his shoulders, his visage beinge of a pale sikelye color.' His piratical activities were pursued mostly along the South Coast, reaching a climax during the autumn of 1581. In early September, he captured the *Anne* of Lulworth in Swanage Bay. Sailing east, he seized a French merchantman, the *Fortune*, off the coast of Brighton. Before the month was out, he had taken a further French vessel in Rye Bay. He then proceeded to waylay other ships over the same stretch of water, causing the mayor or Rye to lodge a complaint that 'none can go forth or come in.' In October, he sailed back to Dorset and was caught at his base in Studland Bay, being imprisoned in Dorchester. The Privy Council announced that 'there is latelye apprehended at Stutland in the Countie of Dorsett one John Piers, a verie notorious pirate borne in Cornwalle, who hathe an olde mother dwelling at Padstowe, noted to be a Wytche, to whom by reporte the said Piers hathe conveyed all such goodes and spoiles as he hathe wyckedlie getten at the Seas.'

Sir Richard Grenville, who lived not far from Padstow at Kilkhampton, was asked to question Piers's mother and 'discover whether she be a Wytche indeed, and what spoiles and goodes she hathe received from her sonne.' He also spoke to the pirate's father William Piers, who was anxious to make clear that he utterly disapproved of John's transgressions and 'had renounced his said sonne for his lewdnesse.' Anne Piers, though, said she had often been on her son's ship and eventually admitted receiving a rug from him. Somebody else confessed to accepting a parrot and a bar of soap. The Searcher of Padstow, John Pentire, told Sir Richard that Piers had once shown him a purse containing nothing but gold coins, also a bag of silver worth at least twenty pounds.

The vicar of Padstow recalled seeing Anne Piers in Bodmin; she had fifteen ounces of plate, which she sold to a goldsmith from Plymouth. Moreover, when Piers was anchored outside Hawker's Cove, people went on board his barque to purchase bolts of calico, the vicar said. Could he remember anybody in particular? Yes, the vicar of St. Merryn.

Sir Richard informed the Privy Council that, as far as he was concerned, Anne Piers hardly qualified as a witch (thus saving her from a burning) and that John Piers's booty was rather less than awe-inspiring.

Meanwhile, the pirate escaped from Dorchester Gaol, but was soon recaptured. He stood trial at Corfe Castle in March 1582, was found guilty and ordered to be executed. A gibbet was erected on the beach at Studland, where he was hanged in front of a vast crowd from all over the Isle of Purbeck. The authorities ruled that his corpse must remain suspended there indefinitely, 'to the terrifying of others for that the same place hathe bene muche frequented and the inhabitantes molested with pirates.' However, during the night after the execution, two pirates rowed silently ashore from their anchorage in Studland Bay, cut down his body and took it out to sea, leaving only the legend that somewhere in the sands of Harlyn Bay, three miles west of Padstow, lies treasure buried by Piers.

2 STEPHEN HEYNES

A second Studland pirate was Stephen Heynes. He came to prominence shortly after the death of John Piers, and his first notable prize, taken off the coast of Normandy in June 1581, was the French merchantman *Esperance*, returning from South America to Dieppe. Its cargo included 400 tons of brazil wood, several hundred bales of raw cotton, 12 puncheons of pepper, 360 parrots and 54 'munkyes, apes and other beastes.' Heynes brought this vessel into Studland, briskly selling items from the deck, then sailed round to Torbay, where the parrots and 'munkyes' again attracted attention.

Two months later, he seized a barque carrying 35,000 fish from the North Sea. In October, he captured a Scottish ship near the Scilly Isles with a consignment of salmon and herring. His next prize, seized near Dartmouth, was the *Anne* of Plymouth, laden with hops, raisins and dyes from Antwerp. A further ship to be taken was bound for Brittany with Spanish wine.

Heynes was a prodigious worker, impatient with those who impeded his progress. If he felt that the captain of a prize vessel was withholding information, he would quickly resort to torture. He appears to have been the first English pirate to employ the technique of setting light to matches jammed under a man's fingernails. But he had other methods. During the late summer of 1582, he intercepted the 300-ton *Salvator* of Gdańsk on a voyage from Lisbon with a hundred tons of salt and spices. The captain, Gregorious Neumann, was badly wounded, being shot in the leg and stabbed in the shoulder. Although he promptly disclosed the whereabouts of a cache of valuables worth £35, Heynes was not satisfied and demanded to know of more treasure. Neumann insisted he had nothing else of value. Heynes threatened torture, but Neumann reiterated his assurance. The pirate instructed two of his men to hold Neumann fast by the arms and, 'taking a rope full of knottes, tied the same abowte his heade.' He then slipped a rod inside the rope and began slowly to rotate it. Before long, he was turning 'soe forceablye that the blode yssued owt rownde abowte his heade, and the said rope broker a sonder.'

Still not convinced, Heynes took another piece of knotted rope and repeated the process. Again the rope burst, and again he replaced it. By now, Neumann was no longer in any condition to know what was going on and certainly incapable of divulging any information. Fortunately for him, he lost consciousness and slumped to the floor. One might imagine the pirate would have left things at that. Instead, he took the purser of the *Salvator* and subjected him to the same torment 'till he hathe broken two cordes abowte his heade.' Next came the cook, whose agonized convulsions were more than Heynes's own hardened crew could endure. 'Sundry of the companie fell on their knees and besoughte Heynes to spare the cooke': they would search the ship high and low for as long as he wished.

Heynes gave way, though he later consigned the Polish sailors to eight days' bondage in the hold on a diet of biscuit crumbs and water while the cargo was being peddled on deck in Studland Bay. Once everything was sold, Heynes destroyed the spars and rigging, released the captives and spoke again with Captain Neumann, who had somehow managed to remain alive. He told him to go to Corfe Castle, state his pitiful plight to the Vice-Admiral of Purbeck and beg for a loan to help him refurbish the *Salvator* so he could sail it back to Gdańsk. He was to give the money to Heynes, or the ship would be burnt. Neumann went to Corfe Castle and, failing to find the Vice-Admiral, tried the Mayor of Poole, but with no luck. Heynes eventually wearied of waiting for him and sailed away without bothering to set fire to the *Salvator*.

Continuing his brigandage, he captured a ship laden with wax and brimstone off Sandown in October 1582 and then a French barque carrying wine near Dungeness. During November he took two more vessels, with cargoes of wine and general commodities, in Whitstable Bay. A few weeks later, he was washed overboard in a storm and drowned.

6
The Irresistible Traitor

Doubtless if ever man was misbegot
It is this Stucley: of a boundless mind,
Undaunted spirit, and uncontrolled spleen,
Lavish as is the liquid Ocean,
That drops his crowns e'en as the clouds drop rain.

THOMAS Stucley was an unprincipled rogue. Lord Burghley, who knew him well, called him 'a defamed person almost through all Christendom, and a faithless beast rather than a man, fleeing first out of England for notable piracies, and out of Ireland for treacheries unpardonable ... Of this man might be written whole volumes to paint out the life of a man in the degree of vain-glory, prodigality, falsehood, and vile and filthy conversation of life, and altogether without faith, conscience, or religion.' Yet so prodigious was his charm that he captivated kings and queens, emperors and popes, dukes and archbishops, as well as hardened seamen.

He was a swashbuckler who thirsted for adventure; he was proud, brave, restless, acquisitive. He appealed greatly to the Elizabethans and became the hero of several ballads, plays and chapbooks. His energy earnt him the nickname 'Lusty'; his vitality beguiled all who crossed his path. Charles Kingsley understood the effect he had on his contemporaries. There is talk of Stucley in *Westward Ho!*, when one of the characters, Will Cary, proclaims, 'I say Stukely was a right good-hearted fellow at bottom.' Despite his wicked deeds, that was how people felt about him. We see him now as a sort of Drake-gone-wrong or flawed version of Raleigh, but, in truth, Drake and Raleigh may have had more in common with Stucley than we choose to recognize.

He was born at Affeton Castle, near Witheridge in mid-Devon, where the Stucleys still reside four centuries later. The date of his birth is not known, but was around 1525. His father, Sir Hugh Stucley, became Sheriff of Devon in 1544, and, interestingly enough, a descendant, Sir Dennis Stucley, held the same post in 1956. There were rumours during Thomas Stucley's lifetime that his true father was Henry VIII, which might explain why he was treated with warmth and respect not only by Queen Mary and Elizabeth I but by European monarchs as well.

During his late teens he saw military service in France, and in his early twenties returned to join the retinue of Protector Somerset. When Somerset was overthrown in 1551, a warrant was issued for Stucley's arrest, but he escaped across the Channel to the French Court near Tours, where Henry II granted sanctuary to this impoverished second son of a Devon knight. He fought for Henry at Metz against the Emperor Charles V of Spain and, a few months later, reappeared in London carrying a letter from the French king to Edward VI beseeching him to pardon his errant subject for supporting Somerset.

Stucley told Edward's ministers that Henry had asked him to forward information which could help the French capture Calais; there

Thomas Stucley in his early twenties.

was also a plan to land at Dartmouth and Falmouth, take Plymouth and march on London. The ministers listened in wonderment. 'We here be amazed how to interpret the tales and judge of the man,' they concluded. Stucley waited eagerly for his pardon and some form of reward. Instead, he was sent to the Tower until the end of Edward's reign.

On his release in 1553, Stucley departed for the Continent, since there was still the problem of his debts. Before leaving, he had an audience with Queen Mary and charmed her into giving him a letter of recommendation to Charles V, upon whom he attended in Brussels. The Emperor assigned him to the Duke of Savoy, one of the finest military leaders of the day. He joined the Duke at St Omer and campaigned with him against the French, winning his friendship and respect. Since the Duke was invited to London for festivities celebrating Mary's marriage to Charles V's son Philip, he suggested his English comrade accompany him. Stucley, however, was worried his creditors would immediately have him imprisoned and wrote to Mary, 'beseeching you to relent my miserable condition' and asking that, because the debts had been incurred in the service of her father, he be 'exempted from all danger and arrest.' Surprisingly, his request was granted; he was given six months' grace and in December 1554 returned to England.

With his soldier's pay at an end and no other income, he decided that a reliable method of acquiring money was to make it himself. This proved highly successful, but, taking a longer view, he plumped for the additional security of marriage to an heiress, which he accomplished within the six-month moratorium, whisking her off to Devon. Meanwhile, sufficient of the counterfeit coinage had accumulated in London to permit the authorities, confident of having accurately identified the source, to issue a warrant for his arrest. Officers from Exeter forthwith set out for Affeton, but when they arrived, he had flown.

He went back to the Duke of Savoy, with whom he soldiered for another two years, playing a vital role as a cavalry commander in the memorable victory over the French at St Quentin in 1557. This triumph answered his military needs for the moment, and soon afterwards he tried his hand at piracy. Having served Charles V so ably in northern France, he now robbed Spanish ships in the Channel. This caused acute embarassment to Queen Mary, particularly since her husband had recently succeeded his father and become Philip II of

Spain. Stucley's depredations were undertaken in a part of the Channel that suggests he was based in Fowey, but of this we cannot be certain. In May 1558 he was required to appear in London to reply to allegations of piracy; in July he presented himself at the court of the Lord Admiral, who dismissed the charges, yet simultaneously imprisoned Stucley's principal associate. In the meantime, nothing further happened about his coining activities of three years earlier, which could have earnt the severest penalty.

With so many constraints placed upon his public enterprises, he now directed his energies into domestic matters. By chance, three relatives had expired within the space of a year, and he made strenuous efforts to derive maximum financial benefit from these calamities. Following the death of his father, he asked Queen Mary to award him most of the estate in order that he might 'be the better able to serve her majesty.' This and a separate ploy to defraud his four brothers came to nothing. The death of his sister Mary's husband provided him with the opportunity of applying for the wardship of her young son, which he somehow managed to obtain. His next step was to seize her house, but she applied to the Privy Council, who ordered him to leave. The third death was that of his wife's wealthy grandfather, of whom she was the sole heir.

It took no more than two years to disburse what the old gentleman had amassed over a lengthy and successful business career. His profligacy became the talk of the capital.

Stucley he presum'd
To spend a hundred pound a day in waste.
The greatest gallants in the land
Had Stucley's purse at their command.
Thus merrily the time away he past.
Taverns and ordinaries were his chiefest braveries,
Golden angels there flew up and down.
Riots were his best delights,
With stately feasting day and night.
In court and city thus he won renown.

By now a more vibrant and ambitious queen had come to the throne. Stucley instinctively understood Elizabeth and her aspirations. Chancing on a current publication, *The Whole and True Discovery of Terra Florida*, he gained an audience with her and suggested he lead an expedition to colonize the new land, which was thought to be in the West Indies. She liked the idea; he was granted a royal patent, a squadron of five ships and three hundred men. In gratitude, he staged on the Thames near Limehouse, and at great expense to others, a dramatic water pageant that the Queen much enjoyed. During their last meeting before his departure, she said, 'I hope I shall hear from you when you are seated in your principality.'

'I will write unto you,' he assured her.

'In what language?'

'In the style of Princes: To our dear Sister,' he replied.

Towards the end of June 1563 he embarked from London. Jean Ribault, author of the tract on Florida that inspired the voyage, had been invited to sail with him, but off Gravesend he jumped overboard and swam ashore, having by then spent sufficient time with Stucley to estimate that Florida was not the main objective. This belief proved quickly correct. When the squadron put in to Plymouth, it not only took on supplies, but unloaded the contents of a foreign merchantman; the quay was soon piled high with Flemish cloth, Gascon brandy, chests of olives and sugar, also cages containing two seasick lions and a leopard.

Stucley then put to sea and, with no thought whatever of Florida, resumed his piracy of five years earlier. He ranged far and wide, throughout the Channel, across to Ireland, and down to the mouth of the Mediterranean. He intercepted Spanish treasure galleons returning

Spanish galleons similar to those captured by Stucley when based on the coast of County Cork.

to Cadiz from the West Indies and Central America; he captured French ships off the coast of Portugal, Dutch ships off Brittany, German ships off County Cork. Into Dartmouth, Falmouth, Waterford and Kinsale he ran cargoes of gold, silver, spices, hides, wine, linen, silk, furs, muslin, flax – anything and everything.

Envoys from Antwerp, Rotterdam, Bordeaux, Bilbao and other European cities made impassioned pleas to Elizabeth's ministers, demanding compensation for their ruined merchants, clamouring that Stucley be stopped. The Spanish ambassador Don Guzmán de Silva remonstrated weekly at court; Philip II wrote personally to the Queen requesting her to discipline this Captain Tomás Estuclay. The English ambassador in Spain, Sir Thomas Challoner, confessed his embarassment. 'I hang down my head with shame,' he reported from Madrid. 'Alas! Though it cost the Queen roundly, let him for honour's sake be fetched in!'

Left with little alternative, Elizabeth instructed Sir Peter Carew to command a squadron and scour the seas: Stucley must be stopped. It did not take Carew long; in March 1565 he caught the pirate in Cork Harbour, his most frequent anchorage.

Stucley's hearing followed a familiar pattern. Heavy and well substantiated charges were laid against him, but these all faded into the background as glowing affidavits from three influential leaders whom he had charmed while in Ireland were presented to the court of enquiry. The three were Hugh Brady, Bishop of Meath; Sir Harry Sidney, Lord Deputy of Ireland; Shane O'Neill, the powerful chieftain of Tyrone. Elizabeth's position in Ireland was so tricky she decided not to do anything that could alienate these men; in addition, Sidney and O'Neill both asked that Stucley be employed to help them in their struggle to oust the Scots from Ulster. On top of this, the Lord Chief Justice of Ireland, Sir Nicholas Arnold, and even Sir Peter Carew threw in their support. And so Stucley was released 'on recognances', which for him meant absolutely nothing.

He at once determined to make of Ireland the principality he may originally have contemplated for Florida. Scooping £6,000 out of his pirate coffers, he purchased from the Knight Marshall of Ireland, Sir Nicholas Bagenal, not only all his vast estates throughout the country, but his position too. A year later, he similarly bought out Captain Nicholas Heron and, apart from picking up more land, acquired the offices of Seneschal of Wexford, Constable of the Castles of Carlow, Leighlin and Ferns, and Captain of the Kavanaghs. When Elizabeth heard of this empire-building, she was appalled and declared all the transactions invalid. In fury at being stripped of his titles, Stucley contacted Philip II, proposing he invade Ireland. As soon as this plot was uncovered, in June 1569, he was arrested and imprisoned in Dublin Castle. He was released four months later owing to insufficient evidence. Reaching the conclusion that he could make no more progress by remaining in Ireland, he began to lay plans for escaping to Spain and in April 1570 sailed from Waterford to Vivero at the head of a miscellaneous collection of dissidents and adventurers.

He was received at the Spanish Court with every sign of respect and consideration. His ideas about the invasion of Ireland were enthusiastically discussed by the King's ministers. But Philip himself, cautious and methodical, would not be rushed into an undertaking that might have unforeseen repercussions. As compensation, he gave Stucley a knighthood and sent him to join his brother Don Juan of Austria in Sicily, where the fleets of Spain, Venice, Genoa, Malta and the Papal States were assembling in the Strait of Messina prior to sailing against the Turks. The ensuing Battle of Lepanto, which took place in the Gulf of Corinth on October 7th 1571, was the last great conflict in which both sides employed oar-propelled vessels. The Christians annihilated the Turks, who lost 15,000 men and 220 galleys. Stucley commanded a Spanish squadron that was among the most conspicuously successful, and his gallant conduct won him golden opinions as a great champion of Christian Europe. He was thus able to break his journey back to Madrid for an audience with Pope Pius V, to whom he fervently suggested a crusade 'in the name of His Holiness' to liberate Ireland from oppressors of the True Church.

His obsession with returning to Ireland, where his dreams had so nearly been fulfilled, occupied the next five years. Apart from a visit to the Netherlands with Don Juan, he spent almost all the time in Madrid and Rome, trying to persuade Philip II and Pius V to furnish him with the men and resources necessary for an invasion. Philip eventually wearied of him, but Pius's successor Gregory XIII succumbed to the Stucley magic and gave him a galleon of eight hundred tons, the *San Giovanni di Battista,* and six hundred soldiers, together with enough weapons to arm five thousand Irishmen. In keeping with the important part he would be playing in Ireland's future, the Pope conferred on him the titles Earl of Wexford and Carlow, Marquess of Leinster, Viscount of the Murroughs and Kinsellagh, and Baron of Ross and Idrone. The hoped-for designation 'Archduke of Ireland' was not forthcoming, although Gregory intimated that it – and more – could follow in the fullness of time. When he learnt of the papal initiative, Philip contributed 20,000 gold crowns.

Psalms were chanted along the quayside at Civitavecchia as the *San Giovanni di Battista* weighed anchor on February 2nd 1578. In the poop stood Lord Thomas Stucley, resplendent in silver and steel, his chest decked with the insignia of Papal Commander and Order of the Knights of St James; beside him fluttered the banner that the Holy Father had given him to plant in Irish soil.

The *San Giovanni di Battista* proved to be unseaworthy, a wallowing, rotting hulk that needed stripping and totally re- caulking; during her long life, she had also shed various masts, shrouds and tackle. Stucley displayed resourceful seamanship in nursing her through the Mediterranean, but, once past Gibralter and into the Atlantic, she gave every sign of taking them all to the bottom. She was so rickety that on one occasion he had to let her run before a storm for a hundred miles back on their course. At length, eleven weeks out of Civitavecchia, he brought her lumbering and leaking up the Tagus and into Lisbon for repairs.

In appealing to King Sebastian of Portugal for help, he encountered that rarity, a personality as compelling and mesmeric as his own. The twenty-four-year-old Sebastian, who lodged then in the great limestone monastery of the Geronimos, was an ascetic and mystic immersed in the martial arts. His sole ambition had long been to lead a mighty crusade against the Muslims, and the moment had arrived – he was about to embark for Morocco. Stucley must come and bring his men! After the infidels had been exterminated, he could have ships and money for Ireland, but at present more urgent business demanded his attention. The Papal Commander went away to consider the suggestion, learnt that the *San Giovanni di Battista* was now deemed unnavigable, and returned to tell the King that he would gladly accompany him.

The armada of seven hundred vessels embarked from Lisbon in June 1578. Simultaneously in London Elizabeth I, having recently learnt of Stucley's arrival in Portugal, ordered Martin Frobisher, at the head of a flotilla of nine men-of-war, to patrol the south coast of Ireland. In Plymouth, John Hawkins was also put on alert, readying his squadron to hoist sail at a moment's notice.

Sebastian engaged the Moors on August 4th at Ksar-El-Kebir, one hundred and fifty miles northeast of Casablanca. The Christian forces, comprising a nondescript assortment of untrained lads and worn-out veterans from Portugal and Spain, together with German and Papal mercenaries, amounted to 18,000. The Sultan Abd-El-Malek deployed 35,000 well-drilled horsemen and 11,000 arquebusiers; although he was killed, his troops overwhelmed and decimated the Crusaders. King Mohammed XI of Fès also perished, and so did Sebastian. Another renowned casualty at 'The Battle of the Three Kings' was Thomas Stucley, who fell in the thick of the fray.

A fatal fight, where in one day was slain
Three kings that were, and one that would be fain.

7
The True and Tragical History of Mr John Oxenham

One of English history's most picturesque moments occurred at ten in the morning on Wednesday February 11th 1573. Francis Drake climbed a giant tree on the Isthmus of Darien and looked back over the Panama coast to the Caribbean, where his ship rode at anchor. Then, turning his head, he saw the Pacific for the first time and vowed he would some day sail both seas.

Following him up through the branches was his lieutenant John Oxenham, who also stared at the distant ocean 'with a wild surmise'; he, too, would ply those waters! Great wealth awaited the man who did, for in the security of the Pacific Spanish treasure ships cruised all the way from Peru unarmed.

Oxenham, who came from South Tawton, near Okehampton, idolized Drake and felt he should be the first to embark on this adventure. After they had plundered Nombre de Dios and returned to England, he waited more than two years for his fellow Devonian to take the initiative, but Drake was absorbed in other more pressing matters. Too impatient to hold back any longer, Oxenham fitted out two vessels, hired fifty-seven sailors and on April 9th 1576 weighed anchor from Plymouth, setting course for Panama. His cargo included two ready-to-assemble pinnaces that were to be carried across the Isthmus. Unlike the methodical Drake, he neglected in his haste to obtain a letter of marque or any sort of official authorization for his voyage and therefore, whether he realized it or not, was bent upon unequivocal piracy.

Reaching the coast of Panama towards the end of June, he captured a few local vessels, concealed his ships in mangrove swamps near Acla, transported one of the prefabricated pinnaces half across the Isthmus and put it together on the banks of the Chucunaque. It was

The Spanish Main.

forty-five feet long, pulling twelve oars a side, and they rowed it into the Gulf of San Miguel, across to the Pearl Islands in the Gulf of Panama, thus becoming the first English crew to sail those peaceful waters. Before long they achieved one of their main objectives and took an Ecuador galleon laden with gold worth £27,000. They met with no resistance, since the Spaniards had neither guns nor swords. Six days later they intercepted a treasure ship from Lima carrying silver bars valued at £45,000.

This was success on a scale that nobody had envisaged, and the challenge now lay in heaving so huge a weight of bullion back across the Isthmus. There was no point in seeking further prizes, although Oxenham could not resist raiding some pearl fisheries before sailing back to the mouth of the Chacunaque. However, word was sent from the fisheries to the Governor of Panama, who promptly dispatched six galleys towards the Gulf of San Miguel, where the pearl fishers said the pinnace was heading. In the Gulf the galleys came across the ransacked treasure ships, whose sailors directed them towards the Chacunaque. But, once into the mouth of the river, the commander of the pursuit party, Pedro de Ortega, was faced with a dilemma, for this was the mouth also of the larger Tuira.

As the confluence of the rivers approached, he decided to go up the Tuira and was already steering in that direction when he suddenly spotted clusters of birds' feathers drifting out of the Chacunaque. Putting the rudder over, he crossed towards the other bank and, scooping his hand in the water, drew out what were obviously pluckings from chickens. He ordered the other five galleys to follow him and entered the lesser river. After four days of almost nonstop backbreaking effort, they rounded a bend, and there was the English pinnace drawn up on the sand, but with only six pirates aboard. Five of these jumped out and escaped into the woods; the other was shot.

Ortega disembarked eighty soldiers and soon picked up the trail. Within a couple of miles they came across a makeshift hut stacked full with the gold and silver. They removed this to the galleys and were rowing down the river when Oxenham and his men appeared and launched an attack. The Spaniards repulsed this with comparative ease; many Englishmen were killed or captured, while Oxenham and the remainder ran off through the woods.

Some of the prisoners were tortured until they confessed the whereabouts of the two ships hidden near Acla. These were located and taken along the coast to Nombre de Dios. In the meantime, the Viceroy of Peru sent a top commander, Diego de Frias, and one hundred and fifty troops to the Isthmus to apprehend Oxenham for seizing the Lima treasure ship. Frias began his search in August 1577 and six months later caught up with the fugitive in the mountains, where he and his men were living off bananas, plaintains and wild hog. They were taken to Panama City. Asked if he had the Queen's licence or that of any other prince or lord, Oxenham replied, 'My sword is my licence.'

Most of the Englishmen were summarily executed, but Oxenham and three others were shipped to Lima and held in prison for more than a year, being tortured for information about further English activities in South America. Oxenham gave them out-of-date details concerning Sir Richard Grenville. He was handed over to the Inquisition, tried for heresy and sentenced to perpetual service in the galleys. Returned to the civil authorities, he was condemned to death for piracy and hanged in November 1580.

During the three years that elapsed between Oxenham's flight into the mountains on the Isthmus of Darien and his execution in Lima, Francis Drake fulfilled his vow and not only sailed the Pacific, but became the first Englishman to circumnavigate the globe, returning to Plymouth with £600,000 of Spanish booty. In February 1579 he raided Callao, eight miles from Lima, having just magnanimously released three Spanish prisoners. At that stage the English were unaware of what had happened to Oxenham. Had he known, Drake would surely have asked for his freedom in exchange for the three Spaniards.

In *Westward Ho!* Charles Kingsley devotes an entire chapter to *The True and Tragical History of Mr John Oxenham of Plymouth,* introducing a beautiful senorita who accompanies him into the mountains after being taken off one of the galleons. This is based on an account given to Sir Richard Hawkins during his imprisonment in Panama in 1594, but has never been corroborated.

8
Lady Killigrew

THE Killigrews were magnates of piracy. From their headquarters at Arwenack House in Falmouth they not only funded, supervised and sometimes lodged West Country pirates, but made their own highly successful sorties. Their first big haul came in 1557 when they seized a galleon off Land's End with a cargo worth £10,000. From that time, they lived in the grandest style and won social eminence. Sir John Killigrew became Vice-Admiral of Cornwall and Captain in Command of Pendennis Castle, exerting strong influence throughout the Peninsula. It was he who built the great house in 1571 near a solitary part of Falmouth Harbour close to the open sea, at the southern end of present-day bustling Arwenack Street. Little remains of a building that was among the finest Tudor mansions in the West, and the family, too, has vanished; the last male Killigrew died in a tavern brawl in Penryn in 1687. But they are rightly remembered in Falmouth – Killigrew Street is another principal thoroughfare – for in founding their own fortunes, they founded those of the town.

Sir John Killigrew established contacts all along the south coasts of Cornwall and Devon, extending his operations as far as Lulworth Cove in Dorset. He knew which of the West Country gentry were interested in putting up capital for pirate ventures; he ensured that Customs officials prospered by sharing his point of view; he purchased, chartered and provisioned ships; he hired and paid the crews; he housed them in appropriate ports of sale and ports of refuge; he organized the storage, transportation and division of plunder; he settled accounts with financial backers. Nobody from outside the West Country thought it strange that he should be seen with pirates and invite them to Arwenack House, since he had taken the precaution of being appointed Commissioner for Piracy in Cornwall.

Wealth and status sustained his independence. On a certain occasion, one of his captains brought a well-laden carrack into Falmouth and found himself alongside a squadron of royal men-of-war at anchor. Sir John, instantly taking in the situation from an upstairs window at Arwenack House, strode down to the Quay and had a retainer row him out to the flagship, where he stepped on board in his capacity as Vice-Admiral of Cornwall. He chatted for some while in private with the squadron's commander, Captain Jones, praising his incalculable contribution to national security, extolling the beauties of Cornwall and finally pressing him to accept as a token of local gratitude an extended fully paid excursion through the county. So off went Captain Jones, a hundred pounds jingling in his pockets.

There was only one instance in which Sir John had to face real difficulties, and that was due to his wife. This formidable woman had piracy in her blood, being the daughter of a gentleman pirate of Suffolk, Philip Wolverston. Glancing from her bedroom window on the morning of January 1st 1583, she saw a Spanish merchantman tied up right in front of the house. A plan soon took shape. She discovered that the 144-ton *Marie* had been on her way back to San Sebastián with valuable merchandise from Northern Europe before being driven into Falmouth by storms. The owners, Juan de Chaves and Philip de Orio, had been on board – de Orio was also captain – and had gone to stay in Penryn while repairs were undertaken, for the masts were down. At that time there was peace between England and Spain, so the two Spaniards had no worries about leaving their ship, though they did take care to moor her opposite the home of the Vice-Admiral of Cornwall.

Most of the crew remained on board, but they hardly amounted to many. Lady Killigrew was able to match their numbers with her own servants, other Arwenack staff and a few hand-picked men from Penryn. She waited till the masts had been replaced, then made her move at midnight on January 7th. The Spaniards were taken by surprise, quickly overpowered and imprisoned in the hold. Having supervised this successful first phase of the operation, she returned to the house, while her men loosed for sea, ran the *Marie* out of Carrick Roads and stood down the Channel. By the time they dropped anchor in Roaringwater Bay on the south-west coast of Ireland, not a single Spaniard remained on board. Much of the cargo was now sold, together with the ship, after which the servants and others took their separate ways back to Falmouth, each bringing items of booty and, if it can be believed, two barrels of gold coins. Everything was safely and efficiently accomplished, arousing no suspicions and devoid of witnesses and evidence. Throughout all this de Chaves and de Orio never budged from their hostelry at Penryn. They proceeded to lay formal complaint before the Commission for Piracy in Cornwall. Accordingly, Sir John conducted an official enquiry, at which a good deal of confused information was presented. Two of Lady Killigrew's senior men, Henry Kendal and John Hawkins, were closely questioned, since word had somehow filtered out from Arwenack suggesting mischief may indeed have been afoot. However, they had alibis: on the evening of January 7th they were at a tavern in Penryn until past midnight; the proprietor Elizabeth Moore confirmed it and remembered 'a-drying one of their shirtes.' The Commission returned an open verdict that the *Marie* had undoubtedly been stolen, but by persons unknown.

The verdict may have suited the Killigrews, but was scarcely designed to reconcile the two Spanish merchants to their probable financial ruin. They went to London to protest, and, as a result, the Lord Lieutenant in the West, the Earl of Bedford, ordered a second enquiry in Penryn, under the joint chairmanship of Clerk of the Privy Council, Edmund Tremayne, and Sir Richard Grenville – two very canny Cornishmen.

At the second enquiry, held towards the end of April 1583, fresh and totally damning evidence was brought to light by the clever interrogations of the investigators. The alibis of Kendal and Hawkins were broken when Elizabeth Moore changed her mind and decided they had not been with her on the night of January 7th. Kendal and Hawkins began losing their nerve under pressure. Small admissions led to larger ones; discrepancies between their answers opened up new lines of questioning, and, before long, Lady Killigrew's name was mentioned. After that, the whole story started to unravel, and her dominant role became apparent. She had been extremely thorough: attempting to induce de Chaves and de Orio to go on board their ship around midnight by sending word to their hostelry that members of the crew were ill; alerting the Governor of St Mawes Castle that the *Marie* would be coming past, and there was no need to hail her; burying in the grounds of Arwenack not only valuable bolts of cloth, but entire, carefully wrapped leather armchairs.

Tremayne and Grenville were left with no alternative; they sent Lady Killigrew, Kendal and Hawkins for trial at the Assizes in Launceston, where all three were duly found guilty and condemned to death. Sir John fought to procure a reprieve for his wife. He obtained the influential support of Sir John Arundell and Sir Nicholas Hals, and spent time in London with his kinsman William Killigrew, a groom of the chamber at Queen Elizabeth's court, in a desperate race to oil the machinery of Government fast enough to save her life. In the meantime, news came from Launceston (where Martin Frobisher was imprisoned for piracy in 1564) that Kendal and Hawkins had been executed within the bailey of the Castle. Then, at the eleventh hour, a pardon was granted, and Sir John was permitted to take Lady Killigrew back to Falmouth.

He died at Arwenack during the following year. The whole episode, in which he originally played no part, came as a terrible shock and cost him dear. He left heavy debts, amounting, it is said, to almost £10,000.

9
The Glittering Career of Captain Easton

PETER Easton was perhaps the most successful English pirate during the reign of James I. Yet we know surprisingly little about him. He is described as a Dartmouth man, but spent his early years as a labourer in Somerset. Before long he went to sea, serving on privateers and pirate ships, picking up expertise in gunnery. He sailed with Captain Richard Robinson of Plymouth in 1607 and 08, then commandeered a captured galleon and seized many valuable prizes.

His ambitions and powers of leadership were so exceptional that he rapidly rose to become what can best be called a pirate admiral, as leader of a squadron of seventeen pirate frigates. In March 1611 he made a noteworthy catch, the *White Swan* of Rotterdam, laden with sixty-two chests of sugar, forty butts of Canaries wine, twelve hogsheads of syrup and ten barrels of conserve. He liked this vessel well enough to have her adapted as a man-of-war, and made her his flagship. His next prizes, taken that summer, were the *Concord* of London and *Philip Bonaventure* of Dover, between them worth £40,000.

Pursued by both the Dutch and English navies, Easton wintered off the coasts of Mauritania and Senegal. He continued to seize Dutch and English merchantmen, some carrying valuable cargoes of ivory and hides, and also looted a Portuguese fort. He then crossed the Atlantic and began to prey on North American shipping. He captured three Spanish brigantines in Chesapeake Bay, cruised up to Newfoundland, near St John's, where he repaired and further armed his squadron, recruiting another hundred men. In the summer of 1612 he put to sea with a crew of five hundred and plundered French, English, Portuguese and Dutch fishing fleets, from which he extracted merchandise valued at over £20,000.

During late autumn he shifted his operations to the coast of

Morocco and, on the way there, intercepted near the Azores a Spanish treasure ship, relieving it of 'good rich bootie.' After another highly profitable winter, he took his heavily freighted galleons and nine hundred sailors across the Mediterranean and tied up in the delightful port of Villefranche-sur-mer, just east of Nice on the Côte d'Azur. To the amazement and dismay of his various crews, this marked the end of his brisk and glittering career as a pirate chief. His final haul was appraised at 850,000 silver lire.

He decided to settle at Villefranche, which was then in the duchy of Savoy, and built himself a palace there. At that time Savoy was engaged in wars with Spain and Mantua. Easton offered his services to Duke Carlo Emanuele, volunteering to equip and command a pirate fleet to harass the Spanish. Instead, he was invited to oversee the artillery offensive against Mantua, which he did with such distinction that Carlo Emanuele elevated him to the rank of marquis, adding an annual pension of around £4,000. Since Easton was possibly worth more than a million pounds, the pension might seem of little consequence, but his eye was apparently still on money, for his next step was to marry a Savoy heiress; he became a convert to Roman Catholicism to facilitate the alliance. This made him even more acceptable at Court, where he was a popular figure, nicknamed 'Il corsaro inglese'. An English visitor who met him during this period reported, 'hee seemeth to have the age of 40 yeares; his countenance is rude and savadge.' We have no record of when he died.

The Villefranche of Peter Easton's time has virtually disappeared, succumbing to the commercial exigencies of the Riviera. However, one building that he probably frequented remains, drawing admirers from throughout the world. This is the fourteenth-century Romanesque fishermen's chapel of Saint Pierre, which over many years stood neglected, used for nothing more than storing of nets. Then it was discovered by the great writer and artist Jean Cocteau, who in 1957 decorated the interior with some of his most beautiful frescoes.

Captain Every, from Daniel Defoe's history of piracy published in 1724.

10
The King of the Pirates

Come, all you brave Boys whose Courage is bold,
Will you venture with me? I'll glut you with Gold!

CAPTAIN Henry Every, who is thought to have written these lines, was the most famous pirate of his day. He sailed to the Indian Ocean, brought off an unparalleled coup and, true to his boast, glutted his crew with gold. Immediately transformed into a figure of legend, he became known as the King of the Pirates. He is said to have married a beautiful Eastern princess 'with great smooth marbly limbs', and, such was his wealth, that he allegedly proposed paying off the National Debt to win Queen Anne's pardon. Biographies of him poured from the presses, Daniel Defoe ghosted some fictitious memoirs, and the Theatre Royal staged a play based on his deeds.

Yet, reliable information about his early, and much later, life is scanty. According to a biography by Adrian Van Broeck published in 1709, he was born at Cattedown, Plymouth in 1653. His father, after service as a seaman, became a successful merchant, acquiring property and land. At ten, young Every (or Avery) was orphaned, and passed into the care of an aunt, Mrs Norris; his legal guardian was an uncle, Bartholomew Knowles. Mrs Norris died four years afterwards, leaving him £500. This legacy and much of his previous inheritance were embezzled by the unscrupulous Knowles, who, wishing to be rid of the boy, sent him to sea under a brutal captain. Every survived the ordeal, managed to transfer to another ship and saw action in the Mediterranean. One account says that he sailed with Vice- Admiral Sir John Lawson, but this seems unlikely since Lawson was recalled from the Mediterranean in 1664 and died the following year, when Every was still twelve. A more believable narrative relates that he was in

Rear-Admiral Sir Edward Spragge's fleet when the Algerian Navy was destroyed in Bougie Bay on May 8th 1671. He received a commendation for his valour, being eighteen at the time.

Returning to Plymouth in March 1672, he learnt that his guardian was dead and his fortune gone. That same month, Charles II declared war on the Netherlands. With no particular expectations ashore, Every re-enlisted, spending the next two years as a foremastman, until the Treaty of Westminster brought hostilities to an end in 1674. Back in Devon again, he persuaded some Plymouth and Totnes businessmen to give him command of one of their trading vessels. Though only twenty-one, he had seven years' maritime experience, a confident, pleasant manner and an imposing, sturdy physique. He now showed he possessed valuable powers of leadership, and, to the increasing satisfaction of his employers, began to display skill as a negotiator. Within a short time, assured of excellent prospects, he felt sufficiently secure to embark on matrimony. But he wooed and won too impetuously; when his spouse gave birth six months after their wedding, he knew the child could not be his. She then confessed that the father was her former lover, an innkeeper. This disappointment had a profound effect on him. He decided to make a fresh start and took passage to the West Indies.

What became of him over the next dozen years is virtually unknown. He is believed to have been in Jamaica, Yucatan and around Campeachy Bay, usually involved with logwood cutting, which was arduous but profitable; the exceptionally hard cedars from that area sold for almost £100 a ton in Europe. Other lucrative local industries were slaving and piracy, and to these he eventually turned. As a slave trader, he made many voyages to the Guinea Cost. He first 'went on the account' in about 1690, when he was thirty-seven, basing his operations in the Bahamas. His career received a boost from the appointment in June 1690 of the spectacularly corrupt 'Colonel' Cadwallader Jones as Governor of the islands. The 'Colonel', after electing himself to the additional posts of Provost Marshall, Colonial Secretary and Treasurer, levied exorbitant taxes and employed known pirates to enforce compliance; in return, he let them do what they liked. Their only obligation was jury service whenever his position was threatened. At one crucial trial, his hand-picked jurors included six pirates, two alcoholics and a recognized pederast.

The 'Colonel' was ultimately dismissed and recalled to England after four glorious years of unbridled jiggery-pokery ranging from embezzlement to the sale of peerages. Every came too and immediately found a job as first mate of the *Charles*, commanded by the boozy Captain Gibson. This and another man-of-war, the *James*, each carrying thirty guns and one hundred and twenty men, had been superbly fitted out by a consortium under the leadership of Sir James Houblon, MP for the City of London and a director of the Bank of England. Unlikely as it may seem, the two ships were being hired by the Spanish Government to protect their commercial interests in Peru from the French. Their own navy was already over-extended, partly through trying to cope with English piracy in the West Indies; and so they came to the City and to Houblon, whose Huguenot family had recently emigrated from France!

The *Charles* and *James* sailed to Corunna to take aboard Spanish officials and receive orders, but Every, hardly believing his luck, had different plans. With support from most of the crew, he assumed command. Captain Gibson, too awash with grog to comprehend what had happened, was put ashore in a longboat, together with fifteen others who opposed the seizure. Every rechristened the ship *Fancy* and, supplemented by aspiring pirates from the *James*, forthwith set sail on May 30th 1694 for the Cape of Good Hope.

Come, all you brave Boys whose Courage is bold,
Will you venture with me? I'll glut you with Gold!
Make haste unto Corunna; a Ship you will find,
That's called the 'Fancy', will pleasure your Mind.

Captain Every is in her and calls her his own;
He will box her about, Boys, before he has done.
French, Spaniard and Portuguese, the Heathen likewise,
He has made a War with them until that he dies.

Farewell, fair Plimouth, and Cat-Down be damn'd;
I once was Part-Owner of most of that Land.
But as I am disown'd, so I'll abdicate
My Person from England to attend on my Fate.

The first port of call in the *Fancy's* famous voyage was the Cape Verde Islands, three hundred miles west of Senegal. Here they captured three English vessels and added nine more volunteers, mostly West Countrymen, to the crew. The next prizes were two Danish ships intercepted in the Gulf of Guinea on their way from Ouidah with cargoes of slaves, ivory and gold; fourteen Danes decided to join the freebooters. After rounding the Cape, Every made for Anjouan Island, southwest of the Seychelles, where he overcame a French pirate brigantine loaded with spoils from the Red Sea. His forces were augmented by forty of the corsairs, together with another twelve Frenchmen from a shipwreck. The *Fancy* was now powerfully equipped, carrying an additional battery of cannon and some seventy extra seamen. Stocks of provisions were high, having been constantly replenished, and in terms of plunder the voyage was already a success.

Every sensed it was in his grasp to achieve something out of the ordinary, to win substantial wealth. His confidence is apparent in a letter of February 1695 that he left at Anjouan for the captain of the next English ship to call at the island. This peculiar document, addressed to 'all English Commanders', enumerates the *Fancy's* complement of men and guns, stating that Every and his crew are 'bound to seek our Fortunes. I have never as yet wronged any English or Dutch, nor ever intend whilst I am Commander.' He suggests that a captain who wants to avoid being attacked by the *Fancy* should make a certain signal. 'I shall answer with ye same, and never molest you for my Men are hungry, stout, and resolute. And should they exceed my Desire I cannott help my selfe. as yett an Englishmans Friend, Henerry Every. Here is 160 odd French armed Men now att Mohilla who wait the Opportunity of getting aney Ship, take care of yourselves.' The letter was picked up by the captain of the *Benjamin* and delivered to the Governor's palace in Bombay.

From Anjouan Every went north to the Gulf of Aden, where he hoped to come across vessels returning to India from the busy port of Jiddah. He captured and removed £50,000 in gold and silver from the *Fateh Muhammed* off the coast of Somalia and pressed on to the mouth of the Red Sea. Lying in wait were several other pirate ships, including some from New England. They, too, were looking for Indian merchantmen, which were often richly laden but poorly protected; the Mogul Empire, in the midst of immense trading success, had overstretched its resources.

Every's moment of good fortune arrived when a veritable leviathan began to appear on the horizon. Vaster than anything the crew had ever seen, this was the largest ship sailing the Indian Ocean and three times the size of the *Fancy*. Called the *Ganj-i sawai*, it was bound for Surat, one hundred and fifty miles north of Bombay, and belonged to the Great Mogul himself. This man, Aurangzeb, aged seventy-seven, was richer by far than any Western ruler; his annual income, approaching three million pounds, was paid in gold, silver, diamonds, emeralds and rubies. Among the gems that found their way into his treasure house was the 280-carat Koh-i-noor diamond, now the *pièce de résistance* of the British crown jewels.

The *Ganj-i sawai* carried six hundred passengers returning from pilgrimage to Mecca and five hundred soldiers and musketeers, the soldiers being armed with scimitars and shields; the ordnance amounted to around sixty guns. Fortification on this scale made travel by convoy dispensable. Every, however, was undaunted and steered straight at the great ship.

The great ship Ganj-i Swai, *captured by Every near the entrance to the Red Sea.*

As soon as he came within range, the *Ganj-i sawai* opened fire, inflicting immediate damage and heavy casualties. But the *Fancy* responded with a broadside that dismantled the *Ganj-i sawai's* mainmast, wreaking such havoc that Every decided to sail alongside and board her. This dangerous manoeuvre took the Indians by surprise, and before long their resistance was extinguished by the pirates' ferocious attack. The soldiers, superior in numbers and equipment, gave a poor account of themselves, since they should have been able to repel the boarders. In addition, the ship's captain Muhammad Ibrahim provided indecisive and dilatory leadership. One report claims that, distraught over what might befall some Turkish slave girls purchased in Mecca as concubines, he rushed into the hold and wasted valuable time by trying to disguise them as men.

The pirates took two days to search the ship from stem to stern. With mounting excitement, they opened crate after crate of gold, silver, precious stones, silks, satins and luxurious fabrics. The gold and silver amounted to £534,000; there were besides, some 100,000 pieces of eight and about an equal number of Venetian chequeens. So staggering a haul, dwarfing usual pirate booties, soon prompted legend and romance. It is told that Every discovered the Great Mogul's daughter on board. He strode to her cabin and threw wide the door. She stood still and silent, staring in proud defiance as, briefly taken aback, he marvelled at her beauty. He stepped forward and began removing her priceless earrings and necklaces. Finally, from around her ebon throat, he ripped the velvet sash on which hung a moleskin jewellery pouch ...

He is supposed to have married the princess, had a son by her, gone to live in Madagascar and ruled a kingdom. As we shall see, none of this happened. The princess-legend evolved because among the passengers was an elderly woman who had distant kinship with the Great Mogul. She was badly treated by the pirates. Many women were raped; some killed themselves to escape dishonour.

When the treasure and a quantity of women had been removed from the merchantman, the *Fancy* set sail, eventually putting into Réunion Island, one hundred miles southwest of Mauritius. After a general division of spoils among the crew, the Danish, French and other foreign pirates disembarked to await vessels bound for Europe, since it was Every's intention to go to the Caribbean. While the ship was being provisioned, he made good use of his time by returning to a former trade and laying in a stock of eighty-seven slaves. Next stop for the *Fancy* after rounding the Cape was the island of São Tomé in the Gulf of Guinea, where Every, despite his new-found wealth, bought supplies with a bogus bill of exchange. He crossed to the Bahamas and, anchoring off Royal Island, dispatched a sloop carrying a gift of £1,000, some elephants' teeth and a letter to Governor Trott in Nassau on New Providence.

Nicholas Trott was Cadwallader Jones's replacement, yet his character was no better. His recent bankruptcy proved advantageous to Every, and Trott, whose salary was £30 a year, gladly accepted the lavish gift, granting the pirate and his hundred followers the freedom of the island and even entertaining them at his home. The date was now April 1696; the *Fancy's* memorable voyage, which had lasted twenty-two months, was over. Every made a present of the ship to Trott, but before the Governor could take possession, she was driven ashore by a gale and wrecked. The drunkeness of those on board thwarted any chance of saving her.

The pirate gang disbanded and dispersed. Many considered settling in Jamaica and offered the Governor Sir William Beeston £20,000 to admit them and procure a general pardon, but he refused. Governor William Markham of Pennysylvania was more amenable, proposing a cover charge of £100 a head. Benjamin Fletcher, Governor of New York, and John Greene, Deputy-Governor of Rhode Island, also declared their willingness to negotiate. Every bought a sloop, the *Sea Flower*, in New Providence and travelled to Massachusetts with a crew of nineteen. He took a liking to Boston, but could transact no satisfactory deals for unloading his huge collection of jewels. There are stories of his burying most of the treasure in places such as Peddocks Island and Spectacle Island in Boston Bay, although it sounds improbable.

He decided to set sail for Europe and towards the end of June 1696 landed at Dunfanaghy in northwest Donegal. From there he is thought to have gone to Donaghadee or Carrickfergus (both in Belfast Lough) and over to Scotland or England; he is also reported to have left from Dublin. He spoke of aiming for Exeter.

By now, the whole world knew of Every's exploits. The plundering of the *Ganj-i sawai* had produced serious repercussions. When the crippled ship at last reached Surat, word of the calamity, principally the murder of pilgrims and violation of women, spread like wildfire. English East India Company stations in Surat, Bharuch, Agra and Ahmadabad were attacked, and only the speedy intervention of

Governor Ahmanat Khan's troops prevented bloodshed. Nevertheless, the English were made to suffer for Every's crimes. Governor Khan arrested the Company's Surat manager Samuel Annesley and sixty-three other employees and imprisoned them until June 27th 1696 – when Every was beaching the *Sea Flower* in Donegal. Several died from ill-treatment. Meanwhile the principal officer of the Company, Sir John Gayer, guaranteed to escort Indian ships through the Gulf of Aden in an effort to keep open the Bombay and Madras stations, which the Great Mogul threatened with closure. The British Government, in response to Indian demands, issued a proclamation for Every's arrest on July 17th 1696. On August 10th the Lord Justices of England put a price on his head of £500, to which the English East India Company added a further 4,000 rupees. A free pardon was offered to all informers.

The first of Every's crew to be taken was John Dann, who crossed from Dublin to Holyhead and went south to Rochester, where an inquisitive chambermaid discovered that his waistcoat was, literally, worth its weight in gold. She went to the parish constable, who seized him early next morning. The mayor decided to hold him in prison after the quilting of his waistcoat was unstitched, disclosing 2,300 Turkish sequins, with a value of over £1,000.

Dann and another pirate, Philip Middleton, who was apprehended shortly afterwards, turned king's evidence; as a result, several more of Every's men were arrested. Six of these appeared at the Old Bailey on October 19th, when prosecuting counsel made clear the significance of the trial:

> Suffer Pyrates, and the Commerce of the World must cease, which this Nation has so deservedly a Share in, and reaps such Advantage by. And if they shall go away unpunished, when it was known whose Subjects they are, the Consequences may be to involve the Nations concerned in War and Blood, to the Destruction of the innocent *English* in those Countries, the total Loss of the *Indian* Trade and, thereby, the Impoverishment of this Kingdom.

However, to the amazement and acute discomfort of both the Administration and the English East India Company, the jury returned a verdict of 'Not Guilty'. In an effort to convince other nations and the Great Mogul of England's best intentions, a fresh trial was held twelve days later, contrary to all normal notions of justice. This time, prosecuting counsel was Sir Charles Hedges, chief judge of the High Court of Admiralty, who delivered a powerful speech stressing again the commercial disasters that await a country universally regarded as 'a Harbour, Receptacle and a Nest of Pyrates.' The new jury did its duty; on November 25th the six men were hanged at Execution Dock, Wapping. Their fate, which attracted widespread attention, gave rise to another popular ballad.

We robb'd a Ship upon the Seas, the 'Gunsway' call'd by Name,
Which we met near the East Indies, and rifled the Same.
In it was Gold and Silver Store, of which all had a Share;
Each Man 600 pounds and more. Let Pyrates then take Care!

Thus for some Time we liv'd and reign'd as Masters of the Sea;
Each Merchant we detain'd and us'd most cruelly.
The Treasures took, we sunk the Ship, and those that in it were
That would not unto us submit. Let Pyrates then take Care!

Now farewel to this wicked World and our Companions too!
From hence we quickly shall be hurl'd, to clear the Way for you;
For certainly, if e're you come to Justice, as we are,
Deserved Death will be your Doom. Then Pyrates all take Care!

Pirates increasingly needed to take care, since the English East India Company, not content with helping to put nooses round their necks, petitioned the Government to dispatch men-of-war to patrol the Indian Ocean. The Company came to rue this request. The Royal Navy could spare no ships; instead, a privateering vessel bristling with guns was sent 'to act against the King's Enemies, and to take Prizes from them as a private Man-of-War, in the usual Manner, and also to fight with, conquer and subdue Pyrates.' While Every's men were being strung up, that vessel had already reached the South Atlantic. It was under the command of a successful New York businessman, William Kidd, who would shortly carve his own niche in history.

Colonial Governors also had to take care. Nicholas Trott was dismissed that same November. He said he let the pirates stay in the Bahamas because the islands could have been attached by the French. Two years later he married an heiress, thereby acquiring 12,000 acres in the Carolinas.

As for the man whose actions exerted such influence over the lives and careers of others, we must take the rest of his story from Daniel Defoe. The great novelist, who always yearned for riches, was so fascinated by Captain Every's feats that he wrote about them on three separate occasions. The first account, produced for the 1719 Christmas market, is the spurious autobiography, describing how Every rules a kingdom in Madagascar, then travels to Istanbul; his purpose is to reach Marseille, 'from whence I intend to go and live in some inland Town, where, as they have perhaps no Notion of the Sea, so they will not be inquisitive after us.' The second text, *The Life, Adventures, and Pyracies, of the Famous Captain Singleton*, appeared six months later and is a novel using much the same material, in which the hero finally returns to England. Neither of these two books presents reliable information about Every. The third narrative, published in May 1724, is in *A General History of the Robberies and Murders of the Most Notorious Pyrates*, written after the author had completely mastered his subject, and recognized as an outstanding work on piracy.

According to the *Pyrates*, Henry Every went to Bideford and settled there using an assumed name. He had already been known both as Benjamin ('Long Ben') Bridgeman and as Henry Bridgeman, so presumably he chose a further alias. Unless his treasure was hidden in Boston Bay, he must have been in possession of a large number of precious stones and metals. There is a rumour that he buried much of this in the cliffs at Beagles Point, south of Goonhilly Downs, Cornwall, where searches continue to this day. However, Defoe says he kept all his booty and contacted dealers in Bristol, who came and examined it. They took away enormous quantities of diamonds and gold, paying some money and promising more once they found buyers.

Weeks passed, then months, and Every heard nothing. He wrote to Bristol and, after some delay, received a small payment. He wrote again, and was again fobbed off with a pittance. Realizing he was being tricked he went to Bristol, confronted them and 'met a most shocking Repulse; for when he desired them to come to an Account with him, they silenced him, by threatening to discover him, so that our Merchants were as good Pyrates at Land as he was at Sea.' Deeply troubled, he fled to Ireland; then, realizing the futility of such an action, he worked his passage back to Plymouth. Utterly destitute, he tramped across Devon to Bideford, where, ill and weary of life, he died, 'not being worth as much as would buy him a Coffin.'

Defoe gives no date for Every's death. In Proclamations of Pardon to pirates of 1698 and 1701, his was the only name to be twice excepted. But this does not prove he was still alive. On the other hand, one authority on piracy, Charles Hill, claims Every reached the age of seventy-five and was buried in the churchyard of St Mary's,

Bideford on June 10th 1728 – although no surviving tombstone or register substantiates this.

Some experts believe he may have settled in London, the largest city in Europe, where a population of half a million would have cloaked him in almost impenetrable anonymity. His crewman John Dann testified that on his way through St Albans he spotted the wife of another pirate, Henry Adams, boarding a stagecoach. He suspected she had transferred her affections to Every; she evidently confirmed this by saying 'she was goeing to Captaine Bridgmans.' She would not reveal her precise destination, but it seemed to be the capital, which could be where Every spent his final years. If he did, he may have attended the play about himself, *The Successful Pyrate*, by Charles Johnson, introduced at the Theatre Royal in November 1712, at the same time that Handel's *The Faithful Shepherd* came on at the Haymarket. The opera received enthusiastic reviews, while Johnson's drama was castigated for 'making a Tarpaulin and Swabber the Hero' and being 'an Encouragement to Villainy and a Disgrace to the Theatre.' However, on the 15th of that month, the base Cornishman Lord Mohun killed the Duke of Hamilton in a duel in Hyde Park and himself expired shortly afterwards, provoking intense public interest. Amid such excitement, Handel's gentle piece (now highly regarded) faded away and was withdrawn. But *The Successful Pyrate* benefited greatly and played to packed houses. It was the sort of good luck that would have brought a knowing smile to Captain Every's weather-beaten cheek.

A 17th century engraving of two Barbary Corsairs.

11
The Barbary Corsairs

1 RAIDERS OF THE WESTERN SHORES

THE Barbary Corsairs erupted from the Mediterranean during the first half of the seventeenth century, wreaking terror on the West Country. Not content with seizing ships, these so-called 'Turkish' pirates carried away seamen and landsmen too. Their bases on the Barbary Coast were the Muslim ports of Tunis, Tripoli, Sallee and Algiers, where the demand for slaves was immense. They made lightning raids along English beaches, rounding up labourers in the fields and dragging families out of home and tavern. They snatched people off the shores of Devon, Cornwall and Somerset, most of whom were never seen again.

In 1617 an entire fishing convoy returning from Newfoundland to Dorset was captured by thirty men-of-war. This brought recent English losses to more than three hundred ships and crews. The wastage reached such proportions that in 1620 James I sent a flotilla to confront the marauders in the Mediterranean, but it proved so ineffectual that the English appeared even more defenceless. In 1622 the Mayors of Lyme Regis and Weymouth reported that those towns had been impoverished by the despoilation of their trading vessels.

The year 1625 witnessed a further increase in Barbary attacks. The Mayor of Plymouth repeatedly informed the King's Council that the south coasts of Devon and Cornwall were in the grip of the Turk. The Governor of the Scilly Isles wrote of 20-gun marauders queuing up off Land's End to enjoy the pickings. The Mayor of Barnstaple confirmed that the north coast of Devon was also under siege. In August the situation deteriorated alarmingly. Sixty men, women and children were snatched from a church near Penzance and carried away. In desperation, the Lizard light was extinguished, for it was thought to benefit Turks more than English. The Mayor of Plymouth now calcu-

A Barbary galley of the 16th century.

lated that a thousand West Country mariners had been enslaved since winter; Looe had lost eighty in the last ten days, and during that time another twenty-seven merchantmen had gone. Ship owners instructed their captains to put in to ports like St Malo and La Rochelle to await orders before braving the Channel. The Mayor of Poole warned that the town's Newfoundland fleet of two hundred and fifty sail, with crews of four thousand, was in jeopardy; within two years His Majesty would have no sailors left.

This high-water mark of Barbary aggression was endured, but Charles I did nothing to help, being preoccupied with his own survival. The raids continued, according to weather and Moorish whim. The next bad year was 1631, when the corsairs fell upon Ireland's southern coast, sacking Baltimore and bearing away a hundred townsfolk. Men and women were also plucked from the shores of Somerset above Weston-super-Mare. Fowey suffered gravely, too, and, like Dartmouth a little earlier, became 'so decayed in shipping, mariners, fishermen, and all sorts of people living by trade, being spoiled by Turks and pirates,' that 'many people have abandoned the town and gone to other places to seek their living.' Such tales of woe were oft repeated as the Civil War swallowed up an increasing number of lives and resources. Not until the coming of the

Commonwealth, with its new leaders and new spirit, were the Turks rebuffed.

In November 1654 Cromwell selected Admiral Robert Blake, from Bridgwater, to take a squadron to North Africa. During the following April the English bombarded Tunis, reducing its twin fortresses to rubble, destroyed an entire corsair fleet, subjected Algiers to similar punishment and brought away hundreds of English, Irish and Scottish slaves. Blake was suitably extolled in verse:

The barbarous pirates upon Tunis strand
Felt the effects of his revenging hand.

This was by no means the end of Muslim presence in English waters, but it much reduced the number of galleymasters who chose to make the long voyage up through the Bay of Biscay. In 1671 the Irish admiral Sir Edward Spragge repeated the treatment. With their fleet smashed to pieces in Bougie Bay, the terrified Algerians executed the Dey and compelled his successor to make peace with Charles II, beseeching Spragge to vouch for their submissiveness. From then on, the Barbary Corsairs stayed mostly nearer home.

The Mediterranean, showing the main Barbary bases.

2 A CHRISTIAN TURN'D TURK

He that's condemn'd to th'oare hath first his face,
Eyebrowes and head close shaven (for more disgrace
Cannot betide a Christian). Then, being stript
To th' girdle (as when roagues are to be whipt),
Chain'd are they to the seates where they sit rowing,
Five in a row together; a Turke going
On a large plancke between them, and though their eyes
Are ready to starte out with pulling, he cryes
'Worke, worke, you Christan curres,' and though none needs
One blow for loytering, yet his bare back bleeds
And riseth up in bunches.

From 'The Lamentable Cries of Prisoners in Algiers under the Turkes' (1624)

When the Barbary Corsiars were at the height of their success, they held about twenty thousand Christians in captivity. That a large proportion of the unfortunate creatures were English, and West Countrymen, is apparent from a petition presented to the Duke of Buckingham in 1626 by 'the distress'd wives of almost 2,000 poor mariners remaining most miserable captives in Sallee in Barbary.' These women, having already petitioned King Charles several times without response, begged the Duke 'in his wonted goodness and gracious pity' to intercede on their behalf. Their husbands were 'suffering such unspeakable misery and tortures that they are almost forc'd to convert from their Christian religion.'

These men and their fellows in Tunis, Algiers and other Muslim strongholds were usually put into galleys or employed as menials. Those assigned to the galleys rarely lasted many months. Naked, chained to a bench, pulling a fifteen-foot oar for sometimes ten hours at a stretch, perpetually under the lash, they remained day and night, week after week at their seats. For food, they received a few rusks and the odd bowl of gruel; for drink, a mixture of water and vinegar with drops of oil. The hot and foetid conditions bred disease. When a rower collapsed over his oar from illness or exhaustion, he was flogged until he returned to his task; if he lost consciousness, he was pitched overboard. A Christian life was of no consequence to the galleymasters.

At market, a slave often fetched the same price as an onion. In domestic service, he would be beaten, starved and even killed. As a civic worker, he might cut stone, dig excavations, build houses, forts and harbours, or empty cesspits. In these jobs his

'Torment of the Slaves', from Histoire de Barbarie (1637).

food was a scanty supply of black bread and decaying olives.

A way of alleviating the torment of such an existence was to forswear Christianity and turn Turk, which resulted in circumcision, leniency, some privileges and improved rations. The best method of all was to be ransomed, though this normally proved difficult to arrange, and few families had the necessary funds. Nevertheless, people regularly returned, thanks often to a community effort. In 1622, for instance, Barnstaple raised £240 and redeemed six local seamen. But it became a matter of luck, depending on the prosperity of one's town. In April 1627 (by which time the Turks were kidnapping Icelanders!) Weymouth reported losses of £26,000, 'including

A Christian turn'd Turk.

relief of the wives and children of those who are slaves at Algiers and Sallee' – the town was no longer in a position to do anything for anybody.

The next year though, a young man ransomed from Algiers was welcomed back to Minehead, reinforcing our impression that the north coast suffered less financial damage than the south. Three and a half centuries later, we might easily imagine how his arrival would have prompted nothing but unalloyed thanksgiving, made all the merrier by his outlandish appearance,

Beclad, belaced, betrimmed, with many knots bespick;
Embroidered, padded, tied; all feathers and all flap;
Curly and queued, equipped, curious of hood and cap.

To improve his chances of survival, he had turned Turk, and here he was in his full Algiers finery for the delectation of friends.

But the matter was rather more serious. As far as the Church and many people were concerned, he was now a Muslim infidel. And so a special service 'for the re-admission of a relapsed', was quickly held at St Michael's in Minehead on Friday March 16th 1628 with a celebrated Somerset clergyman, Dr Henry Byam, officiating in place of the local minister. The young Turk had to stand before the congregation in his Barbary costume while the Reverend Byam declaimed an appropriately weighty oration. 'When I think upon your Turkish attire,' he told the lad, 'I do remember Adam and his figleaf breeches; they could neither conceal his shame, nor cover his nakedness ... How could you hope, in this unsactified habit, to attain Heaven?' But the address rose steadily from the shadows of despair, like a prisoner up dungeon steps, towards the final sunburst of salvation. 'You whom God suffered to fall, and yet of His infinite mercy vouchsafed graciously to bring home, not only to your country and kindred, but to the profession of your first faith, and to the Church and Sacraments again, let me say: Give glory to God, sing praises to Him who hath delivered your soul from the nethermost hell.'

At the moment of readmission, the young man cast off wanton faith and satanic garb; his jellabah and other rum togs fluttered and rustled to the ground, his tarbooṣh went rolling across the flagstones. A Christian reborn, he at last stood clothed only in the purity of his faith.

Life on the Barbary Coast was generally brutal and terrifying for the English, other than a small minority – the renegades. These freebooters offered their services to the Turks as shipwrights, cannon-founders, gunners, navigators and even corsair captains. The Turks had little experience of constructing ocean-going vessels and were deficient in seamanship; their strength lay in their soldiers who far outnumbered the sailors on every man-of-war and were a match for anybody on land or sea.

Most successful of English renegades was the legendary John Ward, who in 1603 at fifty (squat, bald, white-haired) lodged in the back streets of Plymouth, finding occasional work as a deckhand. He then joined forces with some other no-hopers, stole a pinnace and captured a merchantman. In rapid progression they siezed vessels of increasing size, transferring each time to the larger, during which Ward became leader and took them into the Mediterranean. By 1605 he was commanding a 200-ton frigate of thirty-two guns and a hundred men. In the following year he went over to the Turks, made his base at Tunis and achieved ever greater prosperity, marrying a Sicilian girl and building a 'faire palace beautiful with rich marble and alabaster.' Ballads kept pace with his amazing rags-to-riches story.

At Tunis in Barbary
Now he buildeth stately
A gallant palace and a royal place,
Decked with delights most trim,
Fitter for a Prince than him
The which at last will prove to his disgrace.

To make the world to wonder,
This captain is commander
Of four-and-twenty ships of sayl,
To bring in treasure from the sea
Into the markets every day,
The which the Turks do buy up without fail.

Ward became a Muslim, took the name Issouf Rise ('Rise' meaning 'Captain') and reached the age of seventy, dying in the lap of luxury. It is hardly surprising that his life was a spur and inspiration to others.

One such aspirant was another middle-aged small-time Devon ruffian, Henry Chandler, who picked up a few mediocre prizes, made his way to Algiers, convinced the Turks he was a second John Ward and embraced Islam, styling himself Rammetham Rise. He gained command of a captured Bristol merchantman, the *Exchange*, which he fitted out as a man-of-war and crewed mostly with cheap labour: English, French and Dutch slaves – men like carpenter Mustapha (actually William Winter), gunner Jafar (Richard Clarke) and boatswain Mamme (John Browne). He also suffered from the unusual drawback for a West Country sailor of possessing little seamanship. To rectify that, he appointed as navigator an enslaved Plymouth sklipper, John Rawlins. This proved a mistake, for Rawlins was a man of altogether superior attainments with an utter loathing for the Turks.

They set sail in January 1622, shaping course for the Straits of Gibraltar, since the captain's intent was to waylay merchant shipping off the coast of Spain. They were not disappointed, catching several moderately sized vessels. Instead of taking them in tow, Chandler manned each one and sent it back to Algiers, thereby much depleting his own crew and soldiers.

This blunder convinced Rawlins there was a chance to win control of the *Exchange*. With two of the other slaves, Roe from Plymouth and Davies from Fowey, he conceived a plan involving a faulty bilge pump. He informed Chandler that the pump could only be made to function if the ship was trimmed differently fore and aft: she was too much down by the head for the pump to empty the bilges. Rawlins' solution involved shifting a considerable weight astern to bring her bows more out of the water. He suggested every man available go aft and stand on the poop deck. The captain hesitated, then agreed.
The soldiers and most of the crew crammed themselves on to the poop, and Rawlins worked the pump, and Roe and Davies spent the time appropriating as much weaponry from the empty cabins as they could carry. After a relatively few minutes, lest they invite suspicion, Rawlins came on deck and declared the job completed.

As soon as the other slaves had rejoined the three conspirators and promised their support, they were allotted weapons. The attack was made without delay, meeting with little opposition. Some of the soldiers jumped overboard; the rest were thrown into the sea dead or alive. Chandler was manacled and put under guard. Rawlins conducted a brief service of thanksgiving, they sang a familiar psalm, then cleansed the *Exchange* from stem to stern and pointed her for Plymouth, which they reached on February 13th. Two days earlier one of Chandler's captured merchantmen had docked at Penzance. Instead of making for Algiers, the English slave who was navigating had sailed in the opposite direction without the Barbary soldiers realizing anything was wrong. After a cursory trial, Rammetham Rise, alias Henry Chandler, was tried and hanged in Exeter, together with his associates Mustapha, Jafar and Mamme.

4 THE PIRATES OF PENZANCE

The final appearance of Moorish pirates in the West Country occurred in the early hours of Tuesday September 30th 1760, when a large strange ship carrying twenty-four guns ran ashore at Penzance between Wherry Town and Newlyn. Folk poured out of their houses, and, lo and behold, there were the Barbary corsairs again!

Over a century had passed since their last dreaded visit to Mount's Bay, and three-quarters of a century since Sir Edward Spragge routed them at Bougie, and yet they were suddenly back, standing on the beach in tarbooshes and baggy pants, with pistols sticking out of their cummerbunds and scimitars in their hands. Most of the townsfolk were terrified; they turned tail and fled, shouting, 'The Turks are coming! The Turks are coming!'

A volunteer company assembled, marched to the beach and confronted the Muslim horde, who stood stock-still, their black eyes glittering in the moonlight. The Cornish commanding officer stepped forward and spoke quietly to the captain of the frigate, who then addressed his men, following which they laid down their arms.

It transpired that these were indeed the Barbary corsairs, but they never had the slightest intention of coming anywhere near England. The captain and navigator had charted a course that, at the moment they grounded, put them by their reckoning somewhere off the coast of Portugal. The ship was wrecked beyond repair, and eight men lost their lives.

The general feeling in Penzance was that these mariners might well have the plague, which was the sort of thing that went with being foreign. They were therefore removed to The Folly, a large building on the old Western Green, and kept in strict quarantine, attracting such interest that people came from as far as St Ives to glimpse them strolling in the grounds.

Eventually a British man-of-war called at Penzance and took them back to Algiers.

12
Incident at Dartmouth

An incident at Dartmouth on June 7th 1623 involved only two people: the pirate Nutt and the Vice-Admiral of Devon Sir John Eliot.

John Nutt was a fearsome fellow, who rose from humble origins to become a pirate admiral like Peter Easton, though on a less spectacular scale. Born at Lympstone, between Exeter and Exmouth, he went to sea as a gunner on a Dartmouth ship bound for Newfoundland, where he joined other malefactors in seizing a Dieppe galley which he used for further acts of piracy against the French. In so doing, he unwittingly put a stop to France's attempt to wrest the recently established Newfoundland settlement of Avalon from England's tenuous grasp, thus earning the abiding gratitude of the colony's originator Sir George Calvert.

After a profitable spell off the coast of North America, Nutt returned to English waters and built up a pirate fleet based in Torbay. He paid good and regular wages, which was unusual for those times, and employed so many South Devon seamen that royal ships in the area were largely crewed with leftovers.

For more than one reason he was therefore a wanted man. But he never went anywhere ashore without armed bodyguards in sufficient number to deal with practically every sort of threat. Strangely enough for somebody so successful, he decided towards the end of 1622 that he no longer specially wanted to continue with pirating; perhaps he had already made enough money. He applied for a pardon, which he was led to believe would be readily granted. After several months in which the wheels of officialdom revolved with their usual sluggishness, the pardon duly materialized – and was sent to Newfoundland! Dated February 1st 1623 and valid for acceptance within three months, it was completely useless. Unaware of its issue, Nutt proceeded with his piracy, sometimes picking up ten to twelve vessels a week.

Sir John Eliot became Vice-Admiral of Devon in January 1623, a month before the pardon commenced its journey across the Atlantic. A Cornishman from Port Eliot, near Saltash, he was one of the rising stars in the Duke of Buckingham's administration and still no more than thirty years of age. Having entered Parliament as member for his local constituency of St Germans when only twenty-two, he swiftly won Buckingham's approval and was knighted four years later. But he soon developed into a staunch libertarian and powerful orator who eventually made fearless attacks on the autocratic corruption both of Buckingham and of Charles I.

In 1626 he delivered an outstanding speech calling for Buckingham's impeachment and next day was sent to the Tower. When the House of Commons refused to sit until he was released, Buckingham had no alternative but to set him free. However, Eliot lost his office as Vice-Admiral and was imprisoned again in 1627. In 1630 he went to the Tower for the last time, where he wrote four significant works on liberty and government. His health declined so badly that his family begged to remove him to Port Eliot. The King assented to this as long as he recanted, but he refused and died in the Tower in November 1632 at the age of forty. Charles hated him so much that he would not allow his body to be taken back to Cornwall for burial. His harsh treatment of Sir John and his family was decisive in turning the Commons irrevocably against him.

In January 1623, when Sir John moved into the Vice-Admiral's apartments at Dartmouth, all this lay ahead. He was then a typical young man in a hurry. And his main aim was to rid the West Country of John Nutt. The opportunity for doing so came agreeably soon, for the pirate sent word that he was still interested in receiving a pardon, on condition that he be permitted to retain whatever prizes he had taken until the granting of the pardon.

Since Nutt was continuing to inflict severe damage on English commerce – he had just seized the *Edward and John* of Colchester with a cargo worth £4,000 – Sir John decided to act quickly. He travelled to London at the beginning of June and, while making enquiries, chanced on a duplicate of the pardon that had been sent to Newfoundland. He immediately returned to Devon, informing Nutt that the pardon awaited his personal collection, in exchange for a bond of £500 and the nominal surrender of his ships and prizes.

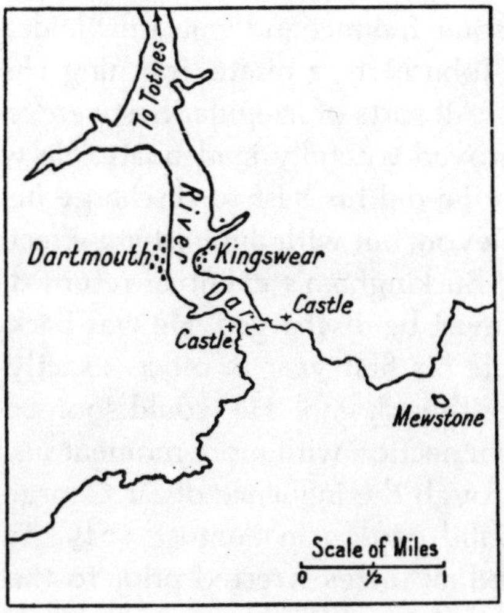

Dartmouth.

Nutt accepted these terms and on the morning of June 7th weighed from Torbay in his flagship *Defiance*, followed by the rest of his fleet with the captured vessels in tow. After clearing Berry Head, he skirted the coast past Sharkham Point and the Mew Stone, sailed up the Dart and cast anchor in Dartmouth Harbour. Minutes later, the two men came face to face. Nutt formally surrendered himself, his crews, ships and goods to the Vice-Admiral and made him a gift of six packs of calfskins. Sir John presented him with the pardon. Then he arrested him.

'But the pardon!' Nutt cried, brandishing it under the younger man's nose.

'It expired five weeks agone,' said Sir John.

The pirate was transferred from Dartmouth Castle to London a fortnight later and held in custody, though not in prison. He instantly contacted Sir George Calvert, founder of the colony of Avalon, who had risen to become Secretary of State to the Privy Council. Sir George had not forgotten the help Nutt once gave him, and he initiated an order summoning Sir John to London. The Vice-Admiral arrived shortly afterwards and, to his dismay, was committed to the Marshalsea Prison.

In the normal course of events, Eliot would have notified Buckingham, who would have ordered his release, but Buckingham was in

Europe. So Sir John languished in confinement until appearing before a board 'to answer some indirect and unjustifiable dealings and practices with one Captain John Nutt, a pirate, touching His Majesty's pardon granted unto him.' All sorts of irregularities were levelled against him, and his defence proved woefully inadequate. He was returned to the Marshalsea, where he did his best to discharge his responsibilities as Vice-Admiral of Devon, but with diminishing effectiveness.

Not until after Buckingham's eventual return did the directive go out that Sir John must be discharged. He was back at Dartmouth just in time to complete his first year in office, exactly half of which had been spent in a Southwark gaol. He would soon be incarcerated there again, though in connection with more momentous matters.

Meanwhile, through the influence of Sir George Calvert, Nutt had been granted a valid pardon in August 1623. This entitled him to retain his ships and all prizes wrested prior to the production of the earlier document that went to Newfoundland. In October he was released from custody and, returning to Devon, repossessed his sundry properties and goods. Before long, he had second thoughts about retiring and, to the delight of his former crews, took to the seas again in the *Defiance*, at the head of his old fleet. However, leaving his wife and children in Paignton, he now ranged more widely, spending much time in Irish waters, where his brother Robert also operated as a pirate. In 1632, the year of Sir John's death, he received another pardon, then captured a merchantman transporting to Dublin the luggage, furniture, wardrobe and plate of Lord Wentworth, Deputy-Governor of Ireland. For a while he joined forces with Algerian pirates to plunder shipping in St George's Channel.

He seems to have enjoyed life away from home, becoming especially keen on Irish girls. According to a reliable source, he once took an attractive colleen off a barque he had seized in Dungarvan Harbour, carried her to his cabin 'and there had her a week.' We do not know what finally happened to him. A report written in December 1635 by Sir Richard Plumleigh, Admiral for the Coast of Ireland, states that he had 'forced from the coast and brought to ruin the English pirate Nutt.' Whether John or Robert, this is the last we hear of either brother.

13
Captain Christopher Condent

CHRISTOPHER Condent of Plymouth became a pirate captain in August 1718. Sailing from the Bahamas as quartermaster on a New York merchant sloop, he first showed his true character by dealing with an Indian deckhand who, weary of being cruelly used, attempted to blow up the ship. The Indian gathered together most of the powder and stacked it forward in the hold. He was on the point of igniting it when Condent, with gun in one hand, cutlass in the other, leapt into the hold. The Indian snatched a pistol from the pile and fired, splintering the quartermaster's cutlass arm, but then fell dead as a return bullet pierced his forehead. According to Daniel Defoe, 'the Crew hack'd him to Pieces, and the Gunner ripping up his Belly, tore out his Heart, boiled and eat it.'

After that, they captured a rather better merchantman than their own. The captain of the sloop decided to change ships and went aboard the prize, taking half the men with him. Elected captain in his place, Condent set sail for Africa, seizing a number of merchant vessels in mid-Atlantic. His greatest success was capturing a Dutch brigantine that had formerly been a privateer. He and his crew transferred to this much superior ship, which they had captured off the Cape Verde Islands, three hundred miles west of Senegal. He renamed her *Flying Dragon* and set course for South America, plundering several Portuguese galleons en route. After putting into the island of Fernando de Noronha, three hundred miles east of Brazil, he resumed his depradations and intercepted cargo vessels from France, Portugal and the Netherlands.

At this time he began to evince a hatred for the Portuguese that found expression in cutting off their ears and noses. Priests and monks were required to say mass at the mainmast, following which the pirates would take turns in climbing on their shoulders

A 19th century engraving of Captain Condent attacking the Indian.

and riding them about the deck in jousts and other sports.

Recrossing the Atlantic, Condent captured merchantmen off the coasts of Guinea and the Congo, rounded the Cape of Good Hope and stood for Madagascar, where he strengthened his crew with other experienced hands. He sailed up to the Red Sea, which he reached a year after leaving the Bahamas. He hoped to emulate Captain Every by waylaying a Mogul treasure ship, but his luck had run out, and nothing presented itself.

The whole of the next year proved equally disappointing, but finally on August 20th 1720 the *Flying Dragon* overhauled in the Gulf of Khambhat an immensely rich Moorish galleon on course from Jiddah to Surat. The crew and passengers of this treasure ship were rewarded for their lack of resistance by being landed on the nearby coast, not far from Bombay. Condent took the prize to the pirate base of Nosy Boraha (then called Sainte-Marie), an islet off north-east Madagascar. Here, they unloaded onto the beach a cargo that surprised everybody by its value, around £162,500. For days they emptied the hold and cabins, heaping upon the sands vast mounds of gold, silver, precious stones, silks, muslins, brocades, velvets, ivory, spices, porcelain, musk and other luxuries. Once the galleon had been emptied, she was sunk.

After this coup, Condent brought his piratical career to a close. The booty was shared out and the *Flying Dragon* burnt. The crew split up, travelling to many points of the compass. Condent went to Mauritius, four hundred and fifty miles east of Madagascar, where he married a Frenchwoman, sister-in-law of the Governor. They lived there a few years, then settled in St Malo, across the Channel from Plymouth.

14
THE TALE OF CAPTAIN AND MRS COBHAM

THE tale of Captain and Maria Cobham is recounted by the outstanding authority on piracy Philip Gosse (1879-1959). Yet one cannot help feeling he may, at best, have knowingly reproduced it from an unreliable source. He claimed a source, but did not disclose it, and nobody else has been able to find it. One must state in his favour that Captain and Mrs Cobham have been heard of in Nova Scotia. The story has no dates, and the Captain lacks a christian name, so it becomes difficult to determine when he and his wife flourished.

There have actually been two pirate captains called Cobham, and it is intriguing that Gosse mentions neither in his writings. The first is Thomas Cobham, an Elizabethan who operated in the Channel with Martin Frobisher around 1565; the second is Nathaniel Cobham, who sometimes joined forces with the Morgans in Jamaica during the 1660s. Nathaniel could be the Captain Cobham of Gosse's story, though it seems unlikely. Thomas does not fit at all.

A final point of interest is that the Duc de Chartres, who appears near the end of the tale, was an intermittent figure in French history; that is to say, the title often lay dormant. It tended also to be a secondary title, its possessor usually being identified by another name, just as the Duke of Rothesay is better known as the Prince of Wales. The story seems to be set in about 1700, when the chronologically nearest Duc de Chartres was Duc Louis-Philippe, who held the title from his birth in 1725 until 1752, when he succeeded his father as Duc d'Orleans. This does not fit either, since he would hardly have been selling his estates before coming of age in 1746.

The story has been placed here after Christopher Condent's because the two have slight similarities.

Cobham, says Gosse, came from Poole and took to smuggling

A pirate woman of the same period as Maria Cobham.

when he was eighteen. He did well, once landing ten thousand gallons of brandy. (Ten thousand gallons is the standard figure for Dorset villains.) Before long, his boat was confiscated, so he bought a cutter in Bridport, mounted fourteen guns and turned pirate. He captured an East Indiaman off the Lancashire coast from which he removed £40,000 of merchandise before sinking the ship and drowning the crew.

The next important event was meeting Maria for the first time, in Plymouth. He persuaded her to sail with him, which caused jealousy among his men until they found she was responsible for having their punishments reduced. Soon after this, Cobham crossed the Atlantic, for British waters had become too dangerous. Making his base in Nova Scotia, he preyed on fishing fleets in the Gulf of Saint Laurence. Many of these were Poole vessels engaged in the highly profitable Newfoundland cod trade. Together with several French pirates, he inflicted such damage that Poole merchants, including the town's Member of Parliament, petitioned the Government to send men-of-war to defend English interests. But no help was forthcoming, and he continued to take many prizes, sometimes disposing of captive sailors by tying them in sacks and tossing them overboard.

Maria took to her new life, dressing like the men, going barefoot on deck in buckskin breeches, calico shirt, and broad leather belt. From her belt were suspended a brace of pistols and a dagger she became increasingly skilled at using. She stabbed to death the captain of a Liverpool brig. She had another captain roped to the windlass, then, after sauntering some several yards away from him towards the cabin house, span round and emptied both barrels into his chest. Some other prisoners, shackled in the hold, she deliberately put to death by feeding them poisoned food.

After a few years, the Cobhams had enough money to retire and settle wherever they pleased. Maria wanted Captain Cobham to purchase a country house on the outskirts of Poole that he had once seen from a distance as a boy, but he felt it would be rash to return to England. Instead, he bought from the Duc de Chartres a sumptuous chateau and extensive lands on the coast near Le Havre, across the Channel from Poole. This estate, which may have been at Deauville, had its own harbour from which Captain and Mrs Cobham went for fishing trips in a ketch manned by members of his former crew. On one such voyage, they came across a West Indiaman becalmed in the Baie de la Seine, and Cobham climbed aboard her to chat with the captain. But his old impulses returned: he drew a gun, shot the captain and summoned his crew from the ketch. Led by Maria, they swarmed onto the ship and quickly overcame all opposition. They sailed their prize down to Bordeaux, where they then sold her.

This was the Cobhams' last act of piracy. Their ensuing decline was as anticlimactic as their rise had been dramatic. Soon afterwards, and out of remorse for leading so sinful a life, Maria committed suicide by taking laudanum. Captain Cobham outlived her by many years, becoming a magistrate and putting on a fair amount of weight.

15
The Pirate who Outsmarted Captain Kidd

I, Captain Cullifoord, while I sailed,
I, Captain Cullifoord, while I sailed,
I, Captain Cullifoord,
Did many merchants board,
Which did much wealth afford, while we sailed.

East Looe in Cornwall has the distinction of being the birthplace of England's most successful homosexual pirate, (see *Captain Kidd and the War against the Pirates,* Robert C. Ritchie). Robert Culliford, who was born there around 1664, sprang to prominence on the night of February 2nd 1690 by stealing the *Blessed William,* a privateer brigantine commanded by none other than Captain Kidd. What makes this act even more preposterous is that it marked his debut in piracy.

Kidd had hired him as a first mate at Nevis in the Leeward Islands, and it was on nearby Anguilla that the young Cornishman persuaded the rest of the crew to sail off with him while the captain was ashore. He could offer them immediate dividends, having located £2,000 booty that Kidd had stored in the hold. From the Caribbean he set course for the Indian Ocean, where most of his piracies were committed over the coming decade.

Eight years later, in May 1698 he brought his ship the *Resolution* into the pirate settlement of Nosy Boraha, off the northeast coast of Madagascar, and then discovered that Captain Kidd was anchored there in the *Adventure Galley*. It was well known that in 1696 Kidd had been commissioned to capture pirates, though since then he had devoted his time increasingly to being one himself. Nevertheless, he ordered his men to take the *Resolution*. However, when they learnt Culliford was commander, they not only refused, but ninety-seven of the crew went over to him, leaving Kidd with less than twenty men.

Culliford invited Kidd aboard the *Resolution*, and the two captains thus met again. Kidd was left with no alternative but to feign friendship, and Culliford took advantage of this by asking if he could spare a few guns and ammunition. As a result, many of Kidd's crew returned and overran the *Adventure Galley*, looting her of anything that took their fancy. Their mood was so fierce that Kidd barricaded himself in his cabin by piling bales of cloth against the door and laid out forty loaded firearms. Had he tried standing up to them, he would undoubtedly have been killed. Shortly afterwards the *Resolution*, now handsomely equipped, put to sea with a hundred and thirty men and forty cannons at her ports. For a second time Kidd was left floundering in Culliford's wake.

Three months later, in conjunction with the *Soldado* (Captain Chivers), Culliford snared the biggest prize of his career, a 600-ton merchantman returning from Jiddah to Surat. Intercepting the ship in the Gulf of Khambhat, above Bombay, the pirates slaughtered many of the crew and passengers, setting a hundred and fifty Mecca pilgrims adrift in boats without oars or sails. The value of the plunder was £310,000. Next year, being wealthy enough to retire, Culliford took advantage of an Act of Grace to surrender in Madagascar to a representative of the Royal Navy on the understanding he would have the King's pardon.

However, owing to various technicalities and the enormity of his recent crimes, he stood trial at the Old Bailey in May 1701 during the same sessions as William Kidd. For political reasons Kidd, who had been commissioned by the previous Whig administration, was the man the new Tory Government were eager to hang, despite the fact that his misdeeds were negligible, particularly compared to Culliford's. Indeed, one of the weightiest points made against Kidd was that he fraternized with the wicked Culliford aboard the *Resolution* instead of trying to capture him. For his part, Culliford cooperated fully with the authorities, informing on virtually every pirate he had come across – and there were many.

On May 8th Kidd was found guilty of piracy and murder and sentenced to be hanged. With justification he protested, 'I am the innocentest person of them all, only I have been sworn against by perjured persons.' On the same day six other pirates were condemned to death for the attack on the Surat merchantman. Of these, one was reprieved: Robert Culliford. He was returned to prison and freed almost a year later on April 9th 1702. What became of him after that is not known.

The unfortunate Captain Kidd hanging in chains near Tilbury after execution at Wapping. He was twice outsmarted by Captain Culliford.

16
The Buccaneer Bishop of Exeter

In 1684 at the age of 25 Lancelot Blackburne was appointed Vicar of Camerton in Somerset. He spent the next forty years in the West Country, becoming Prebendary of Exeter Cathedral in 1691, Sub-Dean in 1694, Dean in 1705 and Bishop in 1717. During his early days at Exeter he was simultaneously Vicar of two Cornish parishes, Calstock and Altarnun. In 1724 he was made Archbishop of York.

Our concern here is not with his ecclesiastical career in England, but with the two years he passed in the West Indies between being ordained at Christ Church, Oxford and taking up his living in Somerset. For, by all accounts, he was a buccaneer!

This may not be quite as extraordinary as it sounds. Religion then played a far fuller role in everyday life, and Blackburne's posting to Antigua in 1682/83 would probably have included some chaplaincy aboard privateering vessels. Moreover, the dividing line between privateering and buccaneering was at that time very thin – we have only to recall the knighting of Henry Morgan by Charles II in 1675. Regarding Blackburne's period in Antigua, Sir Alan Burns has written in his monumental *History of the British West Indies*:

> ... there is nothing inherently improbable in the presence of a chaplain on board a buccaneer ship, as many of the men were religious according to their lights. Père Labat tells the story of a Captain Daniel, a buccaneer (or pirate) who invited a priest whom he had captured to say Mass on board his ship. Guns were fired in salute at the most important parts of the Mass and most of the crew behaved devoutly throughout the service. One man, however, adopted an improper attitude and when he was rebuked by the captain replied insolently with an oath, upon which Captain Daniel immediately drew his pistol and shot the man dead, swearing that he would do the same to anyone else who showed disrespect to the Holy Sacrifice.

Pére Jean-Baptiste Labat, cited here, put to sea with compatriot

French pirates in the West Indies, becoming their chaplain and gunner. He took part in the capture of two English vessels and gave his share of the spoils to charity.

Blackburne may have acted in a comparable capacity. He never denied accusations of a piratical past, yet never supplied details, perhaps understandably, to substantiate it. Antigua was certainly in the midst of buccaneer activity. The famed buccaneer and chronicler Basil Ringrose ended his career on the island and shipped back to England in February 1682 at precisely the moment the young parson was voyaging in the opposite direction.

Other events in Blackburne's life scarcely conspire to depict him as a saintly figure. In 1702 he was obliged to resign his office as Sub-Dean of Exeter Cathedral on charges of adultery. It took two years to persuade Bishop Trelawny to reinstate him. He was also alleged to have had an affair with the wife of the Vicar of Chagford, thereby siring Thomas Hayter, who became Bishop of Norwich and one of his residuary legatees. In Horace Walpole's opinion, he 'had all the manners of a man of quality, though he had been a buccaneer and was a clergyman; but he retained nothing of his first profession except his seraglio.' Nor was he touched with any great piety and once, after barely enduring a tedious confirmation, he forthwith called for pipes, tobacco and liquor to be brought to the vestry.

He died in 1743 at the age of eighty-four, following which there appeared a poem *Priestcraft and Lust, or Lancelot to his Ladies, an Epistle from the Shades*. In his will, he asked Thomas Hayter to destroy all his correspondence; so we are left with little that could throw more light on the character of the man who, it was said, 'gained more hearts than souls'. The most striking momento from his life is a magnificent and decidedly unclerical sword now on display in the senior common room of Christ Church College. No wonder he continued to fascinate people after his death, notably Lord Byron, who was attracted by the apparent duality of his nature and added a lengthy footnote about him to his exciting narrative poem *The Corsair* (1814).

Perhaps the most delightful anecdote relating to him concerns a veteran buccaneer who returned to England in the twilight of his days and, meeting an old crony, inquired, 'What ever became of Lancelot Blackburne?'

'He's Archbishop of York,' said the other.

17
Escapes from Plymouth by French and American Corsairs

1 JEAN BART

JEAN Bart, the most famous of French corsairs, was born at Dunkirk in 1650 of privateer and pirate stock on both sides of the family, his maternal grandfather being known as 'Le Renard de la mer'. Dunkirk then stood at the crossroads of nationalist aspirations. The town was overrun by the Spanish when he was almost two, recaptured by the French six years later and on the same day, June 15th 1658, handed over to the English by Louis XIV in a deal with Cromwell. Louis could never find a place in his heart for Dunkirk and referred to its inhabitants as *capres*, imitating the Flemish word (*kapers*) for pirates. He called them this with good reason: Dunkirk had been Flemish for several centuries, and piracy was its métier. Nevertheless, when the chronically insolvent Charles II offered it back for £400,000 in October 1662, Louis accepted, perhaps having learnt to rue his earlier transaction.

These tumultuous events may have helped mould young Jean into the fearless man of action that he soon became. After acquiring the elements of navigation in a smuggling smack, he trained with the Dutch and French navies before becoming captain of a privateer at twenty-three. On his first cruise in the North Sea he picked up seven prizes, worth around £40,000. During the course of a career lasting fifteen years, he is thought to have captured about two hundred and fifty ships and twice that number of fishing-boats. His extraordinary seamanship, grasp of naval strategy, audacity and courage were such that the French Navy could eventually not do without him, and he was persuaded to rejoin them. He distinguished himself so frequently that in 1691 he was called to Versailles and granted an audience with

Jean Bart (1650-1702).

King Louis. Three years afterwards he was again called to the royal court and invested with the rank of Chevalier of St Louis – equivalent to a knighthood. His most famous feat followed a few months later when his country was on the brink of famine and he led an escort that safely convoyed one hundred and twenty grain ships from Bergen to France, withstanding repeated Dutch onslaughts. For this, a medal was struck in his honour. He was promoted to the level of admiral in 1697 and died in 1702. The main square in Dunkirk is now the Place Jean Bart, at the centre of which stands a fine statue of him by Pierre-Jean David.

Jean Bart had many brushes with the English, most of which ended in his favour. In May 1689, though, he was captured in the Channel, taken to Plymouth and incarcerated, sharing a room with five more Frenchmen. These consisted of another, badly wounded, captain named Claude de Forbin; Forbin's second-in-command, Vaux-Mimars; a doctor and two cabin boys. Paris archives show that in 1689 four thousand English and Dutch vessels were seized by French corsairs, so Bart's Plymouth jailers were in no mood to grant him any privileges. Sometimes it was the practice to lodge corsair captains with families who would keep an eye on them; the only requirement was that these men report each day to the civic authorities. But Bart was put firmly behind bars, with guards on the other side of the door.

Mistakenly, the cabin boys were deemed sufficiently harmless to be allowed out for brief spells. They used the time to good effect, managing to smuggle back a file with which Bart immediately set to work on the iron grille that barred the window of their first-floor cell. During a further short period of release, they carried out his instructions and hurried down to the waterfront in search of a vessel. As luck would have it, they chanced upon a drunken fisherman sprawled in the bottom of his boat. They lifted him gently onto the quay, propped him comfortably against a bollard, his flagon at his side, and rowed away to another part of the docks, where they concealed the boat beneath a secluded wharf.

That same night, which was only the third since his arrival, Bart decided to attempt an escape. The weather was blustery, the sky overcast, and the sentries patrolling the street below were reluctant to brave the gusts of heavy rain and lingered under shelter round the corner. Bart, Vaux-Mimars and the doctor took it in turns with the file and, after frantic bursts of sawing, at last succeeded in severing the bars. Employing the time-honoured expedient of improvising a rope out of bedclothes, shirts and anything else that came to hand, they lowered themselves onto the cobbles – except for the unfortunate Vaux-Mimars, who girth proved too much for the narrow window. After they had safely disappeared down a pitch-black alley, he continued to aid them for several hours, simulating different voices in conversation to deceive the guards.

Bart, Forbin, the doctor and two boys made for the docks as fast as they could without inviting suspicion. Forbin was conspicuous enough already. Directly after capture, dazed and wounded, he had been robbed of his stylish clothes until he was stripped naked; sympathetic English sailors provided him with a pair of outsize ripped breeches, a nightshirt and old woollen bonnet.

The boys found it difficult in the dark to retrace their steps, but, after a number of wrong turns, succeeded in locating the wharf, where the boat was still secured. Bart took the oars, which turned out to be of unequal size and length, and Forbin manned the tiller. The night continued squally, which was to their advantage, and at first no one paid attention to the humble fishing-boat slowly crossing the Sound. However, there were armed sloops cruising at the entrance to the port, and one of these decided to investigate. The captain began to hail them, but Bart immediately shouted in English, 'Fishermen!' and, shipping one of his oars, gave a friendly wave. This apparently proved adequate, for the captain cordially bade them good luck and sheered off without coming close enough to notice the dearth of tackle.

A few minutes later they were past Penlee Point and out into the Channel. The most daunting part of the journey lay ahead, since they intended rowing for France. An obvious place to aim at was Roscoff, one hundred and fifteen miles due south, almost on the tip of Brittany. They had no compass, though, and could run a terrible risk; by straying only 18°W, they would miss land altogether and head into the turbulent vastness of the Bay of Biscay. Bart resolved to steer southeast to compensate for wind, tide or his own possible errors, adding many miles to the voyage.

Jean Bart rowing across the Channel after his escape from Plymouth.

They had two slices of good fortune: the weather soon improved, and Jean Bart proved the possessor of almost superhuman strength and endurance. While his comrades took turns with one of the oars, he rowed continuously with the other, apart from an occasional bite at the rations they had brought. After sixty-four hours, they beached their boat on the Breton coast near the little fishing village of Erquy, seventy miles east of Roscoff. They had come a distance of one hundred and forty-four miles.

From Erquy some local men sailed them along the coast to St Malo. Forbin then hastened to Versailles, where he reported his achievement to Government officials and was given a financial reward. Bart went back to Dunkirk; as the father of ten children, he had other priorities.

Jean Bart in later life.

2 RENE DU GUAY TROUIN

René Du Guay-Trouin was born at St Malo in 1673 and as a lad of sixteen cheered Jean Bart's progress through the town after his return from Plymouth. The son of a shipowner and privateer promoter, he had originally been destined for the priesthood, attending a Jesuit college in Rennes, and continuing his studies at the University of Caen. When his tutors expressed doubts over his suitability for the religious life after the discovery of a series of *affaires scandaleuses*, his father terminated his education and put him to work in the family business.

Soon after Jean Bart's escape, René asked to serve aboard one of his father's privateering ships and quickly displayed extraordinary aptitude and bravery. He was initially too audacious for his own good. During the storming of an English merchantman near Ballinskelligs Bay, County Kerry, he was so determined to be first aboard that he leapt too soon and plunged into the sea. As the ships came together, he faced being crushed to death, but contrived at the last moment to catch hold of a rope and swing clear.

At eighteen, he was given command of his first vessel and a year later, in 1692, a powerful frigate with which he inflicted much damage on English shipping. His letter of marque was granted – incredibly – by the deposed James II, now living at Saint-Germain and scheming as cunningly as once he had ruled. In 1694 René became captain of the *Diligente* privateer, with forty guns and a crew of two hundred and fifty. That April, while unlawfully flying English colours, he sailed through a convoy of colliers escorted by the Plymouth-based *Prince of Orange*, which hailed him and on whom he fired before speeding away. A fortnight afterwards Admiral Sir David Mitchell's Channel squadron caught up with him near the Scillies. The first English broadside hurtled through the *Diligente's* top-hamper and, shattering both masts, sent spars and rigging crashing to the deck. Moments later, a ricochet hit René in the groin, and he collapsed unconscious. His crew thereupon surrendered. The *Diligente* was towed into Plymouth, where the seamen were imprisoned in the Royal Citadel while their wounded captain was accorded parole, lodging with a family.

Still no more than twenty years of age and with striking good looks, he attracted widespread interest and was entertained in the homes of several naval officers. On his honour not to escape, he expected in time to be exchanged for an English prisoner in France.

Rene du Guay-Trouin.

Until his wound was sufficiently healed, he had no thought of taking French leave and was enjoying his comparative freedom, celebrity and, not least, the attentions of Plymouth's young ladies 'avec leurs visages de lait.' To one of these girls, 'an extremely pretty shop assistant', he lost his heart and, with it, all ideas of flight. However, when the *Prince of Orange* put in to port and her captain, Samuel Vincent, learnt of his capture, he demanded René be tried for piracy, acquainting the authorities with the illegal flag and attack on the escort ship. As a result, he was arrested and transferred to the Citadel.

Built during the 1660s on the instructions of Charles II, the Royal Citadel was the first English fortress to declare for William of Orange after his landing at Brixham in November 1688; it occupies the eastern end of the Hoe, commanding the entrance to the Cattewater and Sutton Pool, and in those days was approached by a drawbridge and surrounded by a moat. René was now truly under lock and key, but could receive callers and even entertain them to dinner in what amounted to an apartment rather than a cell. A constant visitor was his sweetheart, whose beauty was evidently so breathtaking that all at the Citadel fell for her. By a wonderful stroke of luck, one of the sentries became so besotted by her that he asked René what he felt his chances were. The Frenchman looked him up and down and said he thought they could be promising.

'Do you really think so?'

'Yes, I do.'

'Well, in that case, would you put in a word for me?'

'*Bien sûr!* Here's what we will do.'

René outlined a plan that had sprung into his mind. He would tell his girl that, alas, their romance was doomed: soon they would be divided by *la Manche,* as well as by the enmity between their countries. But he had found another who already loved her and whom he knew she could come to love. He would describe her new suitor's virtues, his respect and admiration for her, then at once introduce him to her and let them enjoy some moments together. The only drawback was that first meetings were so important, and a prison was not ideal. A friendly tavern, like that in nearby Lambhay Hill, was more suitable, where a woman would be at ease.

The guard pondered this stratagem. Letting René out to go to the tavern presented no difficulty, but could he give his word he would return? René grinned disarmingly. '*Mais oui!*' And so a date was arranged.

Having made many friends in Plymouth, René now quickly contacted a Swedish captain who sold him a single-masted yawl for £35, equipping it with musketry, compass, provisions and other necessaries. The boat was hidden near the western end of Richmond Walk in Mutton Cove, which then lay outside the town. Certain Frenchmen on parole in Plymouth were notified of the escape plan and invited to join the crew and supply changes of clothing.

The appointed day arrived, and everything went perfectly. The guard released René from his room, took him to a side-door, unlocked it and sent him off to the tavern. A few minutes later, the young man was in the arms of his sweetheart, who wept tears of joy for his freedom, tears of sadness at his leaving. As soon as the guard appeared, René took one last embrace, introduced him, then slipped away. The guard's thoughts were of nothing but the woman who now smiled up at him.

In Mutton Cove, the escapees gathered, found the boat, donned fishermen's gear and pushed out into the Tamar. They rowed past Devil's Point and Drake's Island, then hoisted sail as dusk crept over Plymouth Sound. A few half-hearted enquiries from sentries on ships-of-war presented no problem to men who were able to hold up token nets and doff their caps. Leaving the Shag Stone behind on the port bow they stood out to sea in high spirits when the canvas suddenly slackened and simultaneously a frigate bore down upon them. The wind now dropped completely. René, at the tiller, instantly ordered the other four Frenchmen to man the oars. They pulled for dear life and, as the frigate began to lose speed, the yawl gradually drew away. Even while the threat receded, they continued to row strongly; they had been sufficiently alarmed to want to put several leagues between themselves and England. At length, too exhausted to carry on, they collapsed over their oars and fell asleep.

Some hours later they were all suddenly awakened by a violent squall that almost capsized the boat. In the nick of time René let fly the sheet, put the helm a-weather and ran before the wind. However, they had shipped so much water they were in imminent danger of sinking. Everybody baled desperately with his cap and anything else that came to hand, and eventually another crisis was surmounted. The provisions were totally ruined, washed overboard or saturated with sea water, but this seemed a small price to pay. Before long the gale subsided, and after a passage of some fifty hours they sighted the familiar island of Bréhat and entered the harbour of Tréguier, thirty-five miles east of Roscoff. From there they travelled by country cart to St Malo, arriving at the beginning of July 1695. The town acclaimed the young corsair as it had done his hero Jean Bart six years earlier.

René Du Guay-Trouin went on to forge a career that rivalled Bart's. Like him, he ultimately joined the French Navy, reached the level of admiral and received the Order of St Louis. He is thought to have captured three hundred merchant vessels. He continued to wreak havoc on English shipping and, according to one naval historian, 'inflicted more humiliation on our arms than any French seaman before or since.' His greatest feat was to blockade Rio de Janeiro, exacting a ransom from the Portuguese of one and a half million francs.

He died in 1736 at the age of sixty-three. The house where he was born has been faithfully preserved. A statue of him was presented in 1829 by Charles X to the town of St Malo, where it stands at the centre of the Place Du Guay-Trouin. There are statues also at Versailles and Nantes. A comedy by Pierre Barré about his escape from Plymouth was staged in Paris in 1804.

3 JOSHUA BARNEY

Captain Barney then preparing,
Thus adress'd his gallant crew:
'Now, brave lads, be bold and daring!
Let your hearts be firm and true!
This is a proud English cruiser,
Roving up and down the main;
We must fight her – must reduce her,
Tho' our decks be strewn with slain.'

Joshua Barney, who was born near Baltimore in 1759, is one of the most colourful figures in America's maritime history and probably the most famous of his country's native-born privateers (John Paul Jones came from Kirkcudbright). At fifteen he was already a ship's captain and had been to jail in Nice; at sixteen he captured his first English vessel. By the time he was seventeen his exploits had earnt him an introduction to George Washington, with whom he stayed for a week at Mount Vernon twelve years later.

Although a man of action, he took every opportunity to acquire the education he lacked, reading volumes of French and history and attending the debates of Congress in Philadelphia. He eventually won the friendship of Benjamin Franklin and Thomas Jefferson. His career continued to be eventful, taking him all over the Americas and Europe. At one stage he joined the French Navy and rose to the rank of *chef de division*; at another he sailed with pirates in the West Indies. He ended his career as a commodore in the American Navy, then retired to develop fifty thousand acres of forest and meadow he had purchased in Kentucky. He died in Pittsburgh in 1818. Ever since, there has usually been a *Joshua Barney* among the ships of the US Navy.

Barney was an eternal foe of England, which is not surprising for somebody who grew up during the birth of the United States. The number of English ships he defeated or captured is legion. One of them he brought to a standstill by the novel means of firing a crowbar with such accuracy that it soared through all the foresails and weather foreshrouds, shredding them to rags. He was four times captured by the English. On the first occasion he was paroled, and on the second and third exchanged for Royal Navy lieutenants, all these confinements taking place in America. When he was seized for the fourth time Admiral Rodney, who had recently put in to New York from

Joshua Barney.

Barbados, decided he needed to be taught a more lasting lesson and ordered his transportation to England for a term of imprisonment. He sailed on the *Yarmouth* and, along with other troublesome colonists, was stowed five decks down in the lower hold next to the keel, some thirty feet below the water-line. The voyage lasted forty-four days in heavy seas. The prisoners were mostly without light, received poor rations and inhaled foul air. The cramped conditions gradually improved, owing to five deaths.

The *Yarmouth* dropped anchor in Plymouth Sound in December 1780. Twenty-one-year-old Joshua Barney was removed to a prison hulk either in Plymouth Roads or more probably in the Hamoaze, at the mouth of the Tamar, where the first such ships, the *Hector* and *Le Brave*, were moored in 1778. These floating prisons came into existence when the War of Independence eliminated transportation to the American colonies, and dilapidated ships-of-the-line or captured foreign merchantmen were utilized to accommodate the surplus. Life in the hulks was brutish and often short; each ship was packed with half-naked, famished convicts who slept on bare floors running in filth and swarming with vermin. The lower decks were even more polluted, the air so foetid that a candle would not burn. Fortunately for Barney his stay here was brief before he was taken to the official penitentiary for enemy servicemen, the Old Mill Prison, south of Union Street in Millbay.

This formidable establishment consisted of a group of massively constructed stone buildings surrounded by high double walls set twenty feet apart. Iron gates, eight feet high, were manned by sentries, while soldiers patrolled regularly. Barney came to the Old Mill with a reputation for resourcefulness, somebody who needed to be kept under special observation. So zealously was he watched that within a few weeks the guards marched him into the Governor's office on only the vaguest suspicion of preparing an escape, and he was immediately clapped in irons for a month. This convinced him he must thereafter appear as innocuous as possible and attract less attention. Accordingly, during exercise one morning, he pretended to sprain his ankle in landing at leap-frog. Two comrades carried him from the yard, bandaged his leg and fashioned some crutches for him. From then on he limped everywhere with the crutches, seemingly too lame to cope without them. The deception worked admirably; the guards paid him scant heed, assuming he was in no condition to attempt a break-out. Meanwhile, he made friends with a sentry who had served in an English regiment in America and received a particular kindness from some of the colonists. This man was sympathetic towards Americans, and through him Barney acquired an English lieutenant's uniform that he managed to conceal from the warders.

At noon on May 18th 1781 he made his move. While everybody else was filing into lunch, he quickly donned the uniform, throwing over it a greatcoat he had recently taken to wearing. He hobbled into the yard, where a sturdy friend was waiting by the wall. Casting away the crutches, he climbed on his shoulders, sprang to the top of the wall and lay motionless. Finding he was unobserved, he dropped to the ground on the other side, took off the coat and flung it over his arm. He strode towards the gate of the outer wall, which was open. The sentry, who had his back turned, swung round at the sound of his approach and, seeing the uniform, came to attention. Barney affably acknowledged him and walked out into the town.

Fifteen minutes later he had found safety in a house whose address he learnt in prison. He was then taken to a more secure hiding-place, the home of a clergyman who helped American refugees. Two other men were there, Colonel William Richardson and Dr James Hindman, both from Barney's own state of Maryland. Although civilians, they were stuck in England, because nobody would give them passage. Barney told them to go and buy a fishing-smack and he would sail them to France. The purchase was made, and three nights afterwards they stole through Plymouth's waterside alleys, safely reaching the quay where the boat was moored. Barney took the tiller, dressed in a tarpaulin hat and old canvas coat with a length of rope knotted round his middle. After helping him to hoist the mainsail, Richardson and Hindman went below.

Half the entire Channel Fleet under Rear-Admiral Robert Digby was at that moment anchored in the Sound. Barney had to thread his way through a maze of frigates, while dawn began breaking and drowsy midshipmen came on deck. He shouted up cheery Devon-burred good mornings to several of these officers, who surveyed him and his craft with glazed indifference. At last he cleared the Sound, and with the fleet behind him, stood boldly out for the French coast. A lively sea was running – too lively for the gentlemen below – and progress was excellent. Then a sail started looming ominously to starboard, and it became clear that a swiftly moving vessel was in pursuit. This proved to be a Guernsey privateer, which some minutes later came alongside. An officer boarded the smack and asked Barney his business.

'I cannot disclose to you my business,' he responded, untying the rope around his waist, opening his coat and revealing the English lieutenant's uniform. 'My man, I must not be detained. My business is urgent. You must suffer me to proceed, or be prepared to bear the consequences.'

The officer returned to the ship, reporting that Barney was on a secret mission. The captain was unimpressed and decided to question Barney himself.

'I should be sorry to hinder you, sir,' he said, 'if you are engaged in an affair of Government, but I am sure you can grant me adequate proof without divulging intelligence of any moment.'

'I cannot, sir,' Barney assured him. 'Would you have me submit my documents to any who choose to impede my passage?'

The captain eyed him for a few moments. 'I feel I must ask you to accompany me back to England,' he replied.

'As you please, sir, and directly to Admiral Digby's flagship at Plymouth.'

This audacious stroke visibly ruffled the captain's resolve, but he held firm. The two vessels turned about and beat their way back up the Channel, putting into Cawsand Bay in Cornwall, three miles west of Plymouth Sound. No sooner had the captain left for the flagship than Barney took advantage of negligent guards and slipped over the side.

Once ashore, he travelled east towards the Hamoaze and before long found himself in Mount Edgcumbe Park, where he was apprehended by one of Lord Edgcumbe's gardeners and charged with trespassing. He quickly mollified the old retainer, who told him where he could catch a lift over to Plymouth. Shortly afterwards Barney hailed a man taking sheep across in a wherry and went with him at a cost of sixpence. By nightfall he was again at the clergyman's, being joined a little later by Colonel Richardson and Dr Hindman, who had gained release from custody. Thus, after a hectic day of hope and despair, they were back where they started.

Escape by sea from Plymouth was now too risky, since the port would have been alerted. Even while they discussed possibilities at supper, a town crier passed beneath the window ringing his bell and announcing a reward for Barney's capture. A new plan was hatched. Three days later, magnificently attired as an aristocratic dandy – with ruffled shirt, silk stockings, powdered wig and silk hat – he set out for Exeter at midnight in a hired post-chaise. A precise description of him had been circulated, and the sentry who stopped him at the city gate had a copy of it. He thrust his lantern into the carriage until it was no more than a few inches from Barney's face, which he scrutinized intently. But the young man had transformed his appearance so expertly, even using make-up, that the sentry permitted him to continue his journey after a few routine questions.

Reaching Exeter in time to take breakfast, he caught the day's first stagecoach to Bristol. His next stop was London, where he did some sightseeing before resuming his flight. He attended a service in Westminster Abbey, went boating on the Thames and watched George III drive to St Paul's. He then journeyed by stage to Margate and boarded the Ostend mail-packet. His attention was immediately drawn to a splendid landau lashed between the deckhouses; nearby stood four matched greys in makeshift stalls, watched over by three liveried coachmen. He was curious to discover which of the passengers travelled in such luxury, but noticed nobody on deck who seemed to fit the bill. Stepping into the great cabin, he was at once struck by the beauty and elegance of a woman who, like everybody else, was finding it difficult to cope with the appalling weather. Seconds later, she was sprawling on the floor in extreme discomfort. he rushed across the cabin and, taking her in his arms, inquired where her stateroom was. She murmured the number, and he carried her there, instructing a pantryman to mull a cup of wine. The traditional seafaring remedy did much to revive her.

Next morning, she greeted him vivaciously, asking whether his destination lay along the route she would be taking; if it did, she would be delighted to provide him with a seat in her carriage. So this was the owner of the landau! Her objective was Turin. Since he had decided to make for Amsterdam, he accepted the invitation and accompanied her as far as Brussels. Before parting, she invited him to escort her to a mansion in the Belgian capital where he was introduced to one of her admirers, a Count Falkenstein, whom he later discovered to be the Emperor Josef of Austria, brother of Marie Antoinette.

In Amsterdam he made contact with America's Minister Plenipotentiary in Europe, John Adams, who sixteen years later became his country's second President. Through him, he secured a bunk on the *South Carolina*, which sailed for Boston from the Texel on August 12th 1781. During the voyage the ship encountered difficulties; the captain lost his nerve and hid in his cabin. But young Barney took over, as we know from the diary of another wayfarer the artist John Trumbull, who painted the famous *Signing of the Declaration of Independence*.

> The ship became unmanageable, the officers lost their self- possession, and the crew all confidence in them. For a few minutes all was confusion and dismay. Happily for us, Captain Joshua Barney was among the passengers – he had recently escaped from Mill Prison in England. Hearing the increased tumult aloft, and feeling the ungoverned motion of the ship, he flew upon deck, saw the danger, assumed command, the men obeyed, and he soon had her again under control.

Shortly after the Peace of Versailles in September 1783, Barney, now twenty-four and captain of the frigate *George Washington*, again visited Plymouth, en route to Le Havre. Having anchored in the Sound, he threw a banquet on board ship in honour of the clergyman and others who had helped him escape. The *George Washington* was decorated with flags and bunting; lanterns were hung in the rigging to illuminate the deck for dancing. Several English naval officers, including an admiral, came to pay their respects. On the following day, Barney crossed over to Mount Edgcumbe Park to thank the gardener for aiding him in his flight and made him a gift of two guineas. During their chat, he learnt that the sentry who provided him with the lieutenant's uniform was the old man's son.

18
William Dampier, Pirate and Hydrographer

In Room IV of the National Portrait Gallery in Trafalgar Square is a painting by Thomas Murray of the only pirate to be allotted wall-space among Britain's worthies. No other likeness exists; here is our sole visual clue to the mind and character of the most extraordinary adventurer in British history. Beneath the picture was formerly the legend 'Captain Dampier (1651-1715): Pirate and Hydrographer', which must have halted even the briskest gallery-goer. 'Pirate' has now been changed somewhat tamely to 'Circumnavigator', but we are nonetheless likely to be slowed down by the piercing steel-blue eyes that stare out from the canvas. They belong to a man who evidently knows his worth and achievement, yet the look is guarded; he seems conscious that his hard-won fame may be short- lived.

In fact, his reputation has risen steadily, as we have come to perceive the magnitude of his accomplishments and influence. His renown rests primarily on his publications: *A New Voyage Round the World* (1697), *Voyages and Descriptions* (1699) and *A Voyage to New Holland* (1703/9). Their merits have grown clearer over three centuries, establishing him as the first great British travel writer, still unequalled in either acuteness of observation and range of interest. Because he was the first to write about so many faraway lands, his books have retained their immediacy and fascination. But they rank as more than superlative travel literature; they also have scientific importance. His object, he said, was 'to see all Countries and observe the Works of Nature.' He was ceaselessly curious about every facet of the physical world, and dozens of his descriptions – such as *cochineal, bread-fruit, flamingo, avocado pear, yam, typhoon* – passed straight into dictionaries and encyclopedias. A high proportion of these proved so accurate that scientists continue to quote them in scholarly jour-

William Dampier in about 1702.

nals and even wrestle with, rather than dismiss, those that seem problematic. The insects, fishes and plants later named after him testify to the regard in which he is held.

He is seen, too, as a pioneer of scientific exploration, honoured through Dampier Archipelago in the Indian Ocean, Mount Dampier in New Zealand, and the port of Dampier in Western Australia. In hydrography (the mapping of oceans, seas and rivers), his worth is also recognized. *A Discourse of Trade-Winds,* which appears in *Voyages and Descriptions,* is a classic exposition of the system of winds, tides and currents in the Southern Hemisphere; more than a hundred years elapsed before it was subjected to other than minor modifications. The Royal Navy has named a survey vessel after him, for he contributed more to the science of hydrography than any other sailor of his age.

An outstanding navigator, he acted as pilot for the memorable privateering voyage of 1708-11, captained by Woodes Rogers, that returned to England with a profit of £150,000 and the de-marooned Alexander Selkirk, model for Robinson Crusoe.

Defoe drew heavily on Dampier's writings for several of his books, as did Swift; *Gulliver's Travels* is much indebted to 'my Cousin Dampier'. Coleridge's Ancient Mariner, with his 'glittering eye', is another literary creation that leans on Dampier. Yet this 'man of exquisite mind', as Coleridge called him, was also a chronicler of the buccaneers and, for eight years, a buccaneer himself, though with scant pecuniary gain. Following his emergence as an author, he was given command of an exploring voyage. He belaboured his lieutenant with a cane and clapped him in irons, for which he was court-martialled. Later, as captain of a privateer, he distinguished himself by irresolution, cowardice and drunkenness. Glancing again at his portrait, we can see the determined, rather morose set of the mouth. He could be difficult and not always predictable. The diarist John Evelyn found him 'a more modest man than one would imagine', while a junior officer claimed he was 'so much self- conceited he would never hear any Reason.'

William Dampier was born in East Coker, Somerset, and baptized on September 5th 1651. He lost both parents, who were farmers, when he was still a boy. Relatives ensured he had a proper education, lasting until he was about seventeen, and he acquired enough Latin to converse in that language with a priest in Vietnam twenty years later. A youthful pointer to his future powers of observation and deduction was the skill to gauge correctly which local fields were best suited to produce which crops (wheat, barley, maize, rye, etc.). It was hoped he would become a merchant but, on leaving school, he went to sea, 'complying with the Inclinations I had very early of seeing the *world*.' His first trips, from Weymouth, took him to France and Newfoundland, which he thought so cold he vowed never again to visit northern latitudes. He then accepted 'the offer of a *warm Voyage* and a *long* one, both which I always desired' and sailed on an East Indiaman to Java. A year later, he was back in East Coker, staying with his older brother George. In 1673, he saw action on the *Royal Prince*, under Admiral Sir Edward Spragge, in clashes with the Dutch. His physical condition after these engagements were sufficiently poor for him to be transferred to a hospital ship. According to certain authorities, the young William Kidd, also in his 20s, served alongside him on the *Royal Prince* and was with Spragge during the final encounter on August 11th, when the admiral was killed.

Following a lengthy spell at the naval hospital in Harwich, he returned to East Coker to convalesce, making friends with the local squire, Colonel William Helyar, who offered him the post of assistant manager on his family's sugar plantation in Jamaica. He decided to accept, sailing from Gravesend in 1674. On arrival at the plantation, described by an earlier Helyar as 'the piss pot of the island', he discovered that the manager, William Whaley, had no intention of allowing anybody to share in the running of the business and proposed he become a sugar boiler. When Dampier turned down the suggestion, he was allotted odd tasks and errands. After eight months of bad feeling, altercation and even fisticuffs, he quit. Whaley informed Colonel Helyar that the new employee had:

> bin nothing but a plage to me ... Wm. Dampier he and I have had sum words about severall things which belong to the plantation ... In short he is a selfe Conceated young man and one that understands leightle or nothing and one that has bin given to rambling and therefor Cannot settle himselfe to stay long in any place ... he went away to the port to See if he Could gett him a passage home without telling mee a word of it ... he knew nothing of keeping a booke but sum thing I thinck hee understood of sailing which I thincke his mind hangs after still, but since he is gon I am not at all troubled at it and shall never desire his returne againe.

Whaley paid him off with thirty shillings, which was promptly spent in the taverns of Spanish Town.

He soon gained fresh employment in Jamaica, as manager of the estate of Captain Richard Hemings, another planter, but 'I was clearly out of my Element there', and after four months he again resigned. For the next six months he worked on Jamaican coasters. In August 1675 he shipped on board a ketch bound for Campeachy Bay to collect logwood in exchange for sugar and rum. The captain was so incompetent that the return journey lasted thirteen weeks instead of the usual ten days. 'I think never any Vessel before nor since made such Traverses ... In all these Rambles we got as much Experience as if we had been sent out on a Design.' And, since he had started keeping his journal at this time, there was much to be noted and described, including racoons, boobies, swordfish – and crocodiles that 'followed a Canoa, and put their Noses in over the Gunnal, with their Jaws wide open, as if ready to devour the Men in it.'

The trip to Campeachy Bay also opened his eyes to the income that could be made from cutting logwood, and he liked what he saw of the life there. So at the age of twenty-four he joined the logwood cutters in Campeachy, where he stayed for the next four months until a hurricane destroyed everything in sight and put the entire area three feet under water. As a result, 'I, with many more in my Circumstances, was forced to range about to seek a Subsistence in Company of some Privateers then in the Bay. In which Rambles we visited all the Rivers from *Trist* to *Alvarado*; and made many Descents into the Country among the Villages there ...' In other words, he became a buccaneer. Nine months later, having recouped his losses, he was back in Campeachy. A year after that he returned to England.

This initial spell of buccaneering is notable for its brevity; apart from financing his rehabilitation as a logwood cutter, its attraction seems to have been the opportunities for acquiring 'more Knowledge and Experience.' The account of what he saw and learnt did not appear before the public, in *Voyages and Descriptions*, until twenty-three years later, in 1699. A number of passages have frequently been anthologized; one marvels that they were based on the observations of a twenty-five-year-old lad with no scientific training, and rendered into limpid prose by a grizzled buccaneer of forty-eight. Here, wonderfully described, are many creatures new to Europeans like the sloth, armadillo and hummingbird. Of the terrifying yellow snake, 'It is reported that sometimes they lirk in Trees: and that they are so mighty in Strength, as to hold a Bullock fast by one of his Horns, when they happen to come so near that she can twist her self about the Limb of the Tree, and the Horn at once.' Some of the spiders are 'as big as a Man's Fist, with ... two Teeth, or rather Horns an Inch and a half, or two Inches long, and of a proportionable Bigness, which are black as Jett, smooth as Glass, and their small End sharp as a Thorn; they are not strait but bending. These Teeth we often preserve. Some wear them in their Tobacco-Pouches to pick their Pipes. Others preserve them for Tooth-Pickers.'

Dampier returned to England in August 1678 'and at the Beginning of the following Year I set out again for *Jamaica,* in order to have gone thence to *Campeachy.*' Before leaving, he married a girl called Judith, who may have been a lady-in-waiting to Isabella, Duchess of Grafton; she continued to live at the Duchess's home, Arlington House in London. Alas, this is all we hear of her.

After some months in Jamaica, Dampier completed negotiations for the 'purchase of a small Estate in Dorsetshire.' If, as seems possible, the property was bought in partnership with his older brother George, it may have been at North Poorton, three miles southeast of Beaminster. On the point of coming back to inspect it, he was persuaded to undertake a short trading trip to Nicaragua's Mosquito Coast. But when they put into Negril Bay on the western tip of Jamaica for provisioning, the crew jumped ship and joined a buccaneer fleet that was gathering there. Perplexed over what to do, Dampier at length threw in his lot with 'the Privateers'. A few days afterwards, in March 1680, the fleet – seven ships and three hundred men – set sail for Panama. Thus began what 'prov'd to be a Voyage round the World.' He would not see England again for another twelve years.

The buccaneers started by plundering the rich fortress-town of Puerto Bello, through which passed much Spanish treasure, conveyed along a paved causeway stretching hundreds of miles down into South America. When the booty was shared out, each man received 160 pieces of eight. They proceeded to march across the Isthmus of Darien, reaching the west coast thirteen days later. Dampier was among the seventy who acquired canoes from the Indians, rowed fifty miles into the Gulf of Panama and captured a 400-ton vessel, *La Santissima Trinidad.* Eighteen buccaneers were killed and twenty-two wounded. They renamed the ship *Trinity* and sailed for Chile, hoping to raid Arica, where silver from the famous mines at Potosi was warehoused. Drake had looted here a hundred years earlier, but the buccaneers could not repeat his success, losing several men and retreating empty-handed. They quarrelled and split up into groups. In three little boats wrested from the Spaniards, Dampier and forty others sailed and rowed back up the coast to the Isthmus, which they recrossed on foot, covering the 110 miles in twenty-three days. Torrential rain slowed progress through sodden jungles and forests and made their many river crossings extremely hazardous.

In such appalling conditions, only foresight allowed Dampier to protect his notebooks. 'I took care before I left the Ship to provide my self a large Joint of Bambo, which I stopt at both Ends, closing it with Wax, so as to keep out any Water. In this I preserved my Journal and other Writings from being wet, tho' I was often forced to swim.'

After returning to the Caribbean, he sailed for a year with French buccaneers, who proved rather ineffectual. '*French* Seamen were the saddest Creatures that ever I was among ... the biggest part of them never stirr'd out of their Hammocks, but to eat or ease themselves.' He transferred to an English ship and, having shared in a number of prizes, went to live in Virginia. His purpose may have been to convert booty into cash, but he is reticent about his time in the colony, which 'is so well known to our Nation, that I shall say nothing of it, nor shall I detain the Reader with the Story of my own Affairs, and the Trouble that befel me during about Thirteen Months of my Stay there.'

In 1683, he took up buccaneering again. However, 'I shall not trouble the Reader with an Account of every Day's Run, but hasten to the less known Parts of the World, to give a Description of them; only relating such memorable Accidents as hapned to us, and such Places as we touched at by the way.' One might imagine this to be principally a voyage of discovery were it not that there are other accounts available. Among the 'memorable Accidents' he neglected to mention was capturing a splendid 40-gun Danish slaver off Sierra Leone. This constituted neither privateering nor buccaneering, but straightforward piracy flagrantly committed against a friendly country. One report states, 'she was well stored with good Brandy, Water, Provisions and other Necessaries', these latter including sixty black girls. The ship was renamed *Bachelor's Delight*.

After cruising in the Atlantic, the buccaneers rounded the Horn and joined forces with others, sometimes mustering a fleet of ten sail and nine hundred men, and scourged the South American coast for a year, with only moderate success. On one occasion they unwittingly let a vessel carrying 750,000 pieces of eight slip through their fingers while they hunted down its sister ship, whose cargo turned out to be 16,000 lbs of quince marmalade. In the midst of all this pirating, Dampier, with his unquenchable curiosity, observed and made notes about practically everything he saw: salt ponds, ambergris, tornadoes, flying fish, lobsters, penguin-fruit, the dildo tree, turtle grass, racoons, Peruvian architecture, map errors ... He also produced what was to become the first published account of the Galapagos Islands, which compares favourably with Darwin's description 150 years later – and Darwin went there solely as a scientist, sponsored by the Admiralty.

In March 1686 Dampier took the opportunity of sailing with one of the buccaneer ships to the East Indies, 'which was a way very agreeable to my Inclination.' By June they were in the Philippines, where they stayed for six months, assuaging the deprivations of their voyage with drinking and debauchery. Dampier used the time to write

A 19th century depiction of buccaneers carousing.

about the Filipinos, their lives, manners, customs, religion, government, animals, birds and plants. His eye for detail is unwavering.

The Women are fairer that the Men; and their Hair is black and long; which they tie in a knot ... They have very small Limbs. They wear but two Garments: a Frock, and a sort of Petticoat; the Petticoat is only a piece of Cloth, sowed both ends together; but it is made 2 foot too big for their Wastes, so that they may wear either end uppermost; that part that comes up to their Wastes, because it is so much too big, they gather it in their Hands, and twist it till it fits close to their Wastes, tucking in the twisted part between their Waste and the edge of the Petticoat, which keeps it close. The Frock fits loose about them, and reaches down a little belows the Waste. The Sleeves are a great deal longer than their Arms, and so small at the end, that their Hands will scarce go through. Being on, the Sleeve sits in folds about the Wrist, wherein they take great pride ... They have neither Stocking nor Shooe, and the Women have very small Feet. The Woman are very desirous of the company of Strangers, especially of White Men.

The dancing-girls are:

gorgeously apparelled, with Coronets on their Heads, full of glittering Spangles and Pendants of the same, hanging down over their Breast and Shoulders. These are Women bred up purposely for dancing: Their Feet and Legs are but little imployed, except sometimes to turn round very gently; but their Hand, Arm, Head and Body are in continual Motion, especially their Arms, which they turn and twist so strangely that you would think them to be made without Bones.

The next year and a half was spent in progressively fruitless forays throughout Indonesia and the South China Sea, with visits to Cambodia, Taiwan, Thailand, Vietnam and China. He was content to persist with these voyages, since 'the farther we went, the more Knowledge and Experience I should get, which was the main Thing that I regarded.'

On January 5th 1688 Dampier and other buccaneers made history by setting foot in Australia, possibly at King Sound on the west coast, north of what is now Dampier Downs. He went on to become the first Englishmen to write about that country.

New-Holland is a very large tract of Land. It is not yet determined whether it is an Island or a main Continent; but I am certain that it joins neither to *Asia*, *Africa*, nor *America* ... The Inhabitants of this country are the miserablest People in the World ... who have no skin Garments, Sheep, Poultry, and Fruits of the Earth, Ostrich Eggs, &c ... They have no Houses, but lye in the open Air without any covering; the Earth being their Bed, and the Heaven their Canopy ... Their only Food is a small sort of Fish. Sometimes they get as many Fish as makes them a plentiful Banquet; and at other times they scarce get every one a taste: but be it little or much that they get, every one has his part, as well the young and tender, the old and feeble ... the Earth affords them no Food at all. There is neither Herb, Root, Pulse nor any sort of Grain for them to eat, that we saw; nor any sort of Bird or Beast that they can catch ... Some of them had wooden Swords, others had a sort of Lances. The Sword is a piece of Wood shaped somewhat like a Cutlass [a boomerang?].

During the spring of 1688, when he was 36, Dampier decided to have done with buccaneering. A few of his comrades felt the same way and, wishing to part company with the rest of the increasingly drunken, aimless and quarrelsome crew, they had themselves put ashore on Great Nicobar Island in the Indian Ocean. They purchased a native canoe, in which they set out for the north coast of Sumatera, 250 miles away. The flimsy craft proved inadequate in tempestuous seas.

I had a lingring View of approaching Death, and little or no hopes of escaping it; and I must confess that my Courage, which I had hitherto kept up, failed me here; and I made very sad Reflections on my former Life, and lookt back with Horrour and Detestation on Actions which before I disliked, but now I trembled at the remembrance of.

They succeeded in reaching Sumatera after five days of relentless buffeting that they withstood only through the most exhausting effort and vigilance. Three of the eight men later collapsed and died, and Dampier took a week to recover.

Over the next two years he worked aboard local merchantmen, making trips to India and throughout Malaysia. For a further five months he served as master-gunner at Fort St George, Bengkulu, in southwest Sumatera, from which he deserted in January 1691, sailing for England together with a tattoed prince called Giolo, whom he had rescued from slavery and planned to exhibit. Stopping off at Capetown, he made copious notes about the 'Hodmadods'. During a five-day stay at St Helena, several of the passengers fell 'over Head and Ears in Love with the *Santa Hellena* Maids ... The young Women born here are but one remove from *English*, being the Daughters of such. They are well shaped, proper and comely, were they in a Dress to set them off.'

When he docked in England in September 1691, he had been away for twelve and a half years and, in more than a dozen stages, had circumnavigated the globe. He brought with him no pirate chest crammed with booty, no portmanteau filled with gold bars, but only his journals and notebooks. He was obliged to sell Prince Giolo, who soon afterwards died of smallpox in Oxford.

Little is known of Dampier's life over the next six years. He presumably spent some time in Dorset, where in peace and quiet he could have collated his notes and drafted *A New Voyage Round the World*. Published in 1697, this became an instantaneous bestseller, running to four editions in two years. Not since Drake and Cavendish had there been an account of a British circumnavigation, and never before in the first person – as soon imitated by Defoe and Swift in *Robinson Crusoe* and *Gulliver's Travels*. But *A New Voyage* offered much more than the earlier chronicles: there were buccaneering adventures, descriptions of foreign lands and customs, strange animals and plants, and, above all, the dogged survival of one ordinary (and not so ordinary) human being who chose to exist on the margin of society.

A New Voyage brought him to the attention of the Royal Society, recently formed to promote scientific research and encourage inquiry into the natural world. The Society's influential members secured a post for him at the Customs House in August 1697. The Council of Trade and Plantations asked his advice on the Darien Scheme for settling a colony in the Isthmus, thus bringing him into contact with another Somerset man, the great philosopher John Locke, who was one of the Council's commissioners. Dampier made so favourable an impression on all whom he met, including Samuel Pepys (a past President of the Royal Society and Secretary of the Admiralty), that he was appointed leader of an exploring voyage to New Holland, despite his buccaneering record and inexperience of naval command. Meanwhile, in response to public demand, he produced his second book *Voyages and Descriptions*, comprising three parts: *A Supplement of the Voyage Round the World*, *The Campeachy Voyages* and *A Discourse of Trade-Winds*. By the time this appeared in 1699, he was en route to the Far East as Captain Dampier of the *Roebuck*.

The voyage was an unhappy one. Dampier's lieutenant, George Fisher, resented serving under an ex-buccaneer and began quarrelling even before they weighed anchor. He criticized his captain for being too lenient with the crew and not flogging them sufficiently. He accused Dampier of planning to turn the *Roebuck*

A

New Voyage

ROUND THE

WORLD.

Deſcribing particularly,

The *Iſthmus* of *America*, ſeveral Coaſts and Iſlands in the *Weſt Indies*, the Iſles of *Cape Verd*, the Paſſage by *Terra del Fuego*, the *South Sea* Coaſts of *Chili*, *Peru*, and *Mexico*; the Iſle of *Guam* one of the *Ladrones*, *Mindanao*, and other *Philippine* and *Eaſt-India* Iſlands near *Cambodia*, *China*, *Formoſa*, *Luconia*, *Celebes*, &c. *New Holland*, *Sumatra*, *Nicobar* Iſles; the *Cape* of *Good Hope*, and *Santa Hellena*.

THEIR

Soil, Rivers, Harbours, Plants, Fruits, Animals, and Inhabitants.

THEIR

Cuſtoms, Religion, Government, Trade, *&c.*

By *William Dampier*.

Illuſtrated with Particular Maps and Draughts.

LONDON,
Printed for *James Knapton*, at the *Crown* in St *Paul's* Church-yard. M DC XCVII.

The title page of the first edition of A New Voyage Round the World.

into a pirate vessel and of hiring a Spanish sailor to murder him.

He also incited the crew to 'Refractoriness', so that, when the ship was not yet across the Atlantic, Dampier took up the habit of sleeping fully armed on the quarterdeck, 'it scarce being safe for me to lie in my Cabin, by Reason of the Discontents among my Men.' When Fisher broached a butt of beer without permission and was publicly rebuked, he bellowed at Dampier 'a great many ill names, as old Rogue, old Dog, old Cheat, and indeavoured to stirr up the Seamen to a Mutiny.' Dampier's response was to thwack Fisher with his cane and have him locked in his cabin. He then called all hands on deck and challenged them to mutiny, while in the background Fisher could be heard roaring his way through 'all the ill names that he could invent.' No revolt ensued, and Dampier crowned the occasion by further confining his lieutenant with leg-irons. When the ship reached Brazil, he took the irregular, but imaginative, step of handing Fisher over to the astonished Portuguese governor of Salvador, with the request that he be put in the city gaol. This whimsical attempt to establish a Royal navy equivalent for marooning proved entirely successful. Fisher was promptly imprisoned; it took him three months to convince the governor that Dampier's precedent was founded in no known rule, regulation or agreement.

By then the *Roebuck* was approaching the coast of Australia, finally reaching its destination at the end of July 1699. The object of the mission had been 'to meet with some fruitful Lands ... productive of any of the rich Fruits, Drugs, or Spices (perhaps Minerals also, etc.) that are in the other Parts of the Torrid Zone' and to make a survey of the coast, investigating whatever might seem 'beneficial for Navigation, Trade or Settlement.' But the expedition was a complete anticlimax and lasted only five weeks. Nothing was discovered, little was charted. Dampier found the coastline of northwest Australia 'not very inviting, being but barren towards the Sea.' They were running out of food and fresh water, and the cook died. The men 'began to droop; some of them being already to my great Grief afflicted with the Scurvy, which was likely to increase upon them and disable them, and was promoted by the brackish Water they took in last for boiling their Oatmeal.' So disappointing was the visit that seventy years elapsed before another attempt was made, by Captain Cook in 1770, to come to grips with Australia. Dampier's trip is commemorated through Roebuck Bay, Roebuck Downs and Dampier Land, northwest of the Great Sandy Desert; further south is the Dampier Archipelago.

In an effort to find drinking water and food, he sailed to Timor, 350 miles north of Western Australia. After successfully reprovisioning, he cruised round New Guinea, discovering and naming the island of New Britain. Patriotic fervour nearly landed him in trouble with a Dutch outpost on November 5th 1699, when he celebrated twin anniversaries – James I's deliverance from the Gunpowder Plot and William III's disembarkation at Brixham – by discharging full-scale ceremonial salutes. These 26-gun salvos precipitated the visit of an emissary, who was relieved to learn that this was not the start of a Portuguese attack. With characteristic curiosity, Dampier investigated any native settlement he came across, including Manam Island, near what is now Dampier Strait, off northeast Papua, which 'all Night vomited Fire and Smoak very amazingly; and at every Belch we heard a dreadful Noise like Thunder, and saw a Flame of Fire after it, the most terrifying that ever I saw.'

This sightseeing had to be terminated when Dampier discovered that the *Roebuck*, officially classed by the Navy as a fifth-rate vessel, was rotting so badly that she could not remain seaworthy much longer. He accordingly set sail for England, making as fast a time as he dared. Repairs had to be undertaken en route, with leaks springing more and more frequently. On one occasion he directed that timbers be replaced with wedges of salt beef, deeming these virtually impenetrable. He rounded the Cape of Good Hope without too many alarms, touched at St Helena, but the ship then began to deteriorate rapidly. He just managed to reach Ascension Island and anchor in shallow water when the *Roebuck* gave up the ghost and sank. To his great credit Dampier succeeded in saving all the crew. But he was now faced with the task of keeping them alive on a desolate, deserted island until another ship arrived. Fortunately they discovered a spring, an 'Abundance of Goats' and some turtles. Six weeks later, three British men-of-war and a merchantman appeared and anchored in the bay. Thus, during the summer of 1701, he reached England after an absence of two and a half years. On the 23rd of that May, Captain Kidd had been executed and suspended in chains at Tilbury Point, where his rotting corpse swung in the breeze for several months. If Dampier returned via the Thames, he would have had a grim welcome. And he had his own problems, having lost his ship, jettisoned his lieutenant and discovered little about Australia. In June of the following year, he was court-martialled

The Roebuck is attacked off the coast of Papua New Guinea.

'for very Hard and cruell usage towards Lieutenant Fisher in beating him on board ye sd. Ship, and confining him in Irons for a considerable Time, and afterwards Imprisoning him on shore in a strange Countrey.' He was docked his entire pay for the voyage and stigmatized 'not a Fitt person to be Employ'd as comd[r] of any of her Ma[ty] ships.'

But out of all this disappointment came the magnificent *A Voyage to New Holland,* last of Dampier's three books and published in two parts, in 1703 and 1709. Here, in addition to the meticulous and vivid descriptions of faraway peoples and places, is a deepening scientific awareness. He remarks in the preface that, 'however *unfit a Person* I may be in other respects to have undertaken this Task, yet at least I have given a faithful Account and have found *some* Things undiscovered by any before.'

In many instances, Dampier's intuition led him to put down facts that, though they perplexed him, proved of immense future benefit. An example in *A Voyage to New Holland* is the table of compass variations, covering five pages, together with some deliberations which were sufficiently accurate to help the famous navigator Matthew Flinders modify the construction of the ship's compass a century later by the addition of what are now known as Flinders' Bars.

Court-martialled he may have been, but Dampier's stock remained high. Ten months after his apparent disgrace, the fifty-one-year-old ex-buccaneer had an audience with Queen Anne and kissed her hand, following receipt of a Letter of Marque that entitled him to command a privateering mission funded by London and Bristol businessmen. He had charge of two ships, the *St. George* and the *Fame,* captained by John Pulling. At his request, an old shipmate, Edward Morgan, joined the *St. George* to represent the interests of the consortium. Since Morgan was finishing a prison sentence when his name was first mentioned, such a choice is intriguing.

The expedition got off to a disastrous start. Having quarrelled ferociously with Dampier, and while the *St. George* was still provisioning, Pulling weighed anchor and sped away to the Canaries. From there he went to Bermuda, where the *Fame's* voyage concluded with the same violence that marked its beginning, when the ship blew up after a cook brought a lighted candle too close to a brandy vat. Meanwhile Dampier made for Kinsale, just south of Cork, and, finding another vessel, the *Cinque Ports,* in readiness for a privateering voyage, reached an agreement with the captain, Charles Pickering, to join forces. They planned to cruise along the coast of South America and intercept Spanish treasure ships.

The *St. George* and *Cinque Ports* left Ireland towards the end of May 1703, reaching the Cape Verde Islands by October. Pickering did not live long enough to enjoy the fruits of the voyage, dying later near Rio de Janeiro. His lieutenant, Thomas Stradling, assumed command of the *Cinque Ports*, but displayed a singular lack of resolve in their first engagement, against a French merchantman, firing his guns only a dozen times, which so baffled Dampier that he withdrew from the attack. This was later followed by the capture of three Spanish vessels, though they yielded little. Dampier could have removed from one of them a valuable cargo of pitch and tar, but decided that such bulky commodities might prove too troublesome.

Our knowledge of what happened on this voyage comes largely from a book written four years later by William Funnell, an officer on the *St. George*. He had no regard for Dampier and portrayed him unsympathetically. Dampier later responded with an eight-page *Vindication*, rebutting Funnell's 'chimerical' accusations, which in turn prompted *An Answer to Captain Dampier's Vindication* by another member of the crew, John Welbe. Balancing these three against each other, we must conclude that the expedition was consistently troubled and that much of the unease stemmed from Dampier's quirkiness, intractability and buccaneering instincts.

While the ships were being cleaned at the island of Juan Fernandez, off the coast of Chile, forty-two men went ashore and refused to continue. Only after prolonged talks did they re-embark. The reconciliation was shortlived, and, following another acrimonious bout of wrangling at the island of Taboga in the Gulf of Panama, Dampier and Stradling parted company. The assorted seamen chose to sail with whichever captain they found the less obnoxious. The *Cinque Ports* went back to Juan Fernandez, where Alexander Selkirk, having gladly quit Dampier, now found he could not stomach Stradling either and had himself marooned there. Stradling travelled north again, wrecked the *Cinque Ports* in the Mapella Islands, was captured by the Spanish and locked in a dungeon in Lima for five years.

Dampier stayed in the Gulf of Panama, picking off local craft and raiding the mainland. Engagements with larger vessels ended in fiasco. According to Funnell and Welbe, their captain was a continuous disappointment. The man who, in *A New Voyage Round the World*, had professed, 'I did ever abhor Drunkeness', was frequently drunk himself and even in the thick of battle would retire to his cabin, posting a sentry outside to ensure he was not disturbed. Welbe writes of one encounter that

> none of our Men quitted their Posts, during the Time of Engagement, except Capt. Dampier himself, who the whole Time of Engagement, neither encourag'd his Men, nor gave any regular Command, as is usually required from a Commander at such Times; but stood upon the Quarter-Deck behind a good Barricado, which he had order'd to be made of Beds, Rugs, Pillows, Blankets, etc. to defend him from the small shot of the Enemy ...

In disgust at what they regarded as lack of resolve, twenty- five of the crew, led by the ship's carpenter, stole away in a forty-ton prize vessel and went to the East Indies, taking with them half the *St. George's* provision casks and much of the ammunition.

Somewhat surprisingly, in view of of his string of uninterrupted failures, Dampier decided to attack the annual Manila treasure galleon bound for the Mexican port of Acapulco. On December 6th 1704 the great ship was espied, gunports closed, unaware of danger; the captain mistook the *St. George* for an auxiliary sent to meet her. Now was the moment to unleash as may broadsides as possible before the huge cannons could be manned and primed. Instead, to the bewilderment of his crew, Dampier ran up the English ensign and let off a single warning shot. This provoked uproar among his officers and complete inaction aboard the *St. George*. During the hiatus, the Spaniards mounted their 18 and 20-pounders and opened fire with such vehemence that Dampier immediately gave the order to stand off. The galleon glided on towards Mexico. Thus, in only a few minutes, treasure reputed to be worth 16 million pieces of eight had come and gone without being threatened.

For half the crew, including Morgan, Funnel and Welbe, this was the final straw. They considered the expedition to be futile and at an end. Seizing a recently captured ten-ton barque that was employed as a guard ship, they set off for home, after Morgan had appropriated most of the loot. They reached Ambon, in the Moluccas, where they were imprisoned as pirates by the Dutch. It is ironic that, having parted from Dampier because of their low opinion of him, they now used his name to secure their release. Dutch translations of *A New Voyage Round the World* and *Voyages and Descriptions* had been published at the Hague as early as 1700, and Dampier the writer and navigator was becoming known across Europe. The Dutch authorities put them on cargo vessels returning to The Netherlands, whence they found passage to England. While in Amsterdam, Morgan sold two magnificent solid silver dinner services that he somehow contrived to keep from Dampier's attention and out of the accounts.

After the fashion of Dampier's ships, the *St. George* now proved to be falling apart, 'eaten like a Honey-comb ... in some Places in the Hold, we could thrust our Thumbs quite through with ease.' For a while, Dampier cautiously confined his operations to the coasts of Colombia and Ecuador. He could attempt little, for his forces had been reduced to twenty-seven. At length, he captured a small Spanish ship in which he crossed the Pacific, abandoning the *St. George* in the Gulf of Panama. He reached England towards the close of 1707. At 56, he had completed his second circumnavigation, but again returned minus his ship, and minus a generous assortment of sister ships, prize vessels, captains, lieutenants, crewmen and booty. The failure of the four-year undertaking confirmed him 'not a Fitt person to be Employ'd as comd^{r}' and did nothing for him financially. The backers, whose losses were substantial, instructed their solicitors to prepare a case of fraud against him.

By good fortune another privateering expedition was being planned in Bristol. This was a highly professional affair with no expenses spared. The syndicate boasted the mayor of Bristol, an ex-mayor and more than a dozen prominent citizens, including some connected with Dampier's 'late disastrous Voyage.' They selected as commander twenty-nine-year-old Woodes Rogers, a Poole man living in Bristol who gave promise of becoming an exceptional leader and administrator. He asked for Dampier as navigator, considering him best qualified in the world to take the post of 'Pilot for the *South-Seas*'. The investors agreed, and inevitably the fraud case was dropped – also, Dampier was in no position to recompense them. He was pleased, at such a comparatively advanced age, to be chosen for this role, which carried officer status and the right to a worthwhile percentage of any profits.

There were two ships, the *Duke*, of 320 tons with 30 guns, and *Dutchess*, 260 tons and 26 guns. (Two hundred and fifty years later the survey vessel HMS *Dampier* would displace 1,600 tons!) Rogers was a disciplinarian and insisted on having double the usual complement of officers. The combined crews amounted to 330. Dampier sailed with Rogers in the *Duke*, whose second-in-command was one of the principal investors, Dr Thomas Dover, an immensely successful physician, well versed in quackery, the inventor of Dover's Powder, a palliative based on opium, whose addictive properties secured him a steady income. The *Dutchess* was captained by Stephen Courtney, a gentleman-adventurer, also an investor, but a proficient officer. The entire nature of the expedition was unlike anything Dampier had experienced on the high seas, not least the morning and evening prayers for ship's company.

The two frigates weighed from Bristol in August 1708. Their ultimate goal was to capture, in about fifteen months' time, the very same Manila-Acapulco treasure ship that had so easily eluded Dampier. In the meantime they intended picking up anything that presented itself. This secondary aim was fruitfully realized, several encounters producing valuable prizes. However, the most memorable episode during the outward passage had nothing to do with privateering. It took place at the island of Juan Fernandez and was described by Woodes Rogers in his book *A Cruising Voyage Round the World*, published in 1712.

> We put out a Signal for our Boat, and the *Dutchess* show'd a *French* Ensign. Immediately our Pinnace return'd from the shore, and brought abundance of Craw-fish, with a Man cloth'd in Goat-Skins, who look'd wilder than the first Owners of them. He had been on the Island Four years and four Months, being left there by Capt. *Stradling* in the *Cinque-Ports*; his Name was *Alexander Selkirk*, a *Scotch* Man, who had been Master of the *Cinque-Ports*, a ship that came here last with Capt. *Dampier*, who told me that this was the best Man in her; so I immediately agreed with him to be a Mate on board our Ship ...
> At his first coming on board us, he had so much forgot his Language for want of Use, that we could scarce understand him, for he seem'd to speak his words by halves. We offer'd him a Dram, but he would not touch it, having drank nothing but Water since his being there, and 'twas some time before he could relish our Victuals ...'

Thus did Defoe find the inspiration for Robinson Crusoe.

As they sailed up the west coast of South America, the *Duke* and *Dutchess* became increasingly successful. In April 1709 off Peru they seized vessels of 260 and 450 tons. A little later Rogers led his forces in capturing the port of Guayaquil in Ecuador, releasing it for ransom of 30,000 pieces of eight. While ashore, many contracted a malignant fever that in eleven instances proved fatal, undermined by Dr Dover's homicidal bloodletting remedy: five pints per man (half the normal human capacity). By now, Rogers could no longer endure Dover, who had succumbed to delusions of grandeur ('When I took by Storm the

Alexander Selkirk being taken aboard the Duke *after his rescue.*

two Cities of Guaiaquil ...' he wrote twenty years later), and transferred him to the *Dutchess*.

That winter Dampier piloted the expedition to the precise point where he had met the Manila galleon five years earlier. In due time the great ship appeared on the horizon, and Rogers prepared for action.

I order'd a large Kettle of Chocolate to be made for our Ship's Company (having no spiritous Liquor to give them); then we went to Prayers, and before we had concluded were disturb'd by the Enemy's firing at us. They had Barrels hanging at each Yard-Arm, that look'd like Powder Barrels, to deter us from boarding 'em. About 8 a clock we began to engage her by our selves ... we gave her several Broadsides, plying our Small Arms very briskly, which they return'd as thick a while, but did not ply their great Guns half so fast as we ... she soon struck her Colours two thirds down. By this time the *Dutchess* came up, and fired about 5 Guns, with a Volley of Small Shot, but the Enemy, having submitted, made no return.

During this engagement, Rogers received a shot through the cheek; 'the Bullet struck away great part of my upper Jaw, and several of my Teeth, part of which dropt down upon the Deck, where I fell.' Yet, lying in a pool of blood, he continued to control operations until the moment of victory.

Not since Cavendish's coup in 1587 had a Manila galleon fallen to the English. This present prize, the *Nuestra Señora de la Encarnación y Desengaño*, surpassed all expectation; every barrel, bale and crate was crammed with riches: gold, silver, uncut diamonds, rubies, Chinese porcelain, beautiful painted fans, musk, cinnamon, cloves, satins, damasks, taffetas, chintz. Quantities were vast: the silk amounted to 45,000 lb.

At 58, an age reached by few buccaneers, Dampier had finally achieved his dream – the prospect of wealth. And there might have been more, since, a few days later, a second galleon hove into view. But she was a new ship carrying additional protective cladding and ordnance of 60 12-pounders. The *Duke* and *Dutchess* engaged her for seven hours, making little headway. Woodes Rogers was again severely injured, losing half his heel and having his foot laid bare to the ankle; once more he commanded while lying on the quarterdeck. The fight was called off when English losses reached twenty. By then, ammunition was low, and the *Dutchess's* rigging was flapping in shreds.

Woodes Rogers, from a stamp of the Bahamas. In later life he became Governor of the Bahamas, and died there in 1732.

Setting out for home, the convoy crossed the Pacific. Dampier demonstrated his remarkable navigational skills by piloting them 6,000 miles direct to the tiny island of Guam, which he had visited in 1686. They sailed on to the Philippines, Java, round the Cape of Good Hope, then revictualled at St Helena and Ascension before anchoring in the Thames on October 14th 1711.

When accounts for the *Duke* and *Dutchess* voyage had been finalized, profits totalled £148,000, with Dampier's share £1,500, assuring him security for life. Litigation among the backers prolonged payment for four years, but financiers were happy to advance credit. So, having circumnavigated the world for a third time and reached the age of 60, he at last retired to a house in Coleman Street, immediately to the east of Moorgate in the City of London. There, 'an old man driven by the Trades to a sleepy corner', he was looked after by his cousin Grace until his death three and a half years later in March 1715. We do not know where he was buried.

William Dampier's diversity and extraordinary range of achievements were somewhat overlooked. For nearly two hundred years after his death there existed no memorial to him, since we do not normally erect monuments to buccaneers. But in 1908 St Michael's, East Coker, where he was baptised, finally put up a magnificent brass plaque depicting him with two of his ships. Mincing no words, its opening lines proclaim:

To the memory of
WILLIAM DAMPIER
Buccaneer, Explorer, Hydrographer

In this same church, the ashes of T. S. Eliot were interred on Easter Saturday 1965. Though neither born nor resident in the village, the Nobel Laureate wished to be buried there because of a distant family connection. His own plaque is across the aisle from Dampier's. Such juxtaposition would have tickled both their fancies.

19
THE WORLD'S FAVOURITE PIRATE

Fifteen men on the dead man's chest –
Yo-ho-ho, and a bottle of rum!

WHO is the world's favourite pirate? If a vote were taken, the winner might well be a man who never actually existed – Long John Silver, in Robert Louis Stevenson's *Treasure Island*. But a vote for him would surely be a vote for Robert Newton, since our idea of Long John is invariably based on that great actor's unforgettable performance.

Appropriately enough, Robert Newton was a West Countryman, born in Shaftesbury, Dorset, on June 1st 1905. He came from a talented family, with Cornish blood inherited from his mother, a writer. His father was a painter, a Royal Academician whose works are in the Tate Gallery and other museums throughout the world. He executed several murals for the *Queen Mary*, on which Robert later drank his way across the Atlantic. He is the only R.A. to have painted an inn sign, out of gratitude for a memorable evening, and to be allotted a room in Buckingham Palace after deciding that the Mall could best be depicted from a royal vantage point.

Robert, who had his father's originality, left school at fifteen, after talking Sir Barry Jackson into giving him a job with the famous Birmingham Repertory Company. By the age of nineteen he was appearing at Drury Lane. He soon graduated to leading roles; then, eager for adventure, he sailed to Canada and became a cattle rancher in British Columbia. Two years later, the lure of the theatre returned. He went back to top parts in London and New York, where Noel Coward chose him to take over from Laurence Olivier in *Private Lives*. During the mid-30s he ran the Grand Theatre in Fulham for three years, directing and usually acting in a new play every week.

Robert Newton as Long John Silver.

His screen career began in 1937, but was interrupted when, with the outbreak of war, he volunteered for the Royal Navy. By that time, he had worked on a number of films with his friends Laurence Olivier and Vivien Leigh and also been in *Jamaica Inn* (1939) and *The Green Cockatoo* (1940). He served on minesweepers for nearly three years before being invalided out because of chest trouble. He resumed filming in Noel Coward's *This Happy Breed* (1944), directed by David Lean, which was followed, notably, by Olivier's *Henry V* (1945) and Carol Reed's *Odd Man Out* (1947). His first extraordinary portrayal, as the terrifying Bill Sikes in David Lean's *Oliver Twist* (1948), was created when he was forty-three and in his twenty-fifth movie. With this performance he earnt star status and at last found himself as an actor.

Two years later came *Treasure Island* (1950) and one of the saltiest, juiciest slices of histrionics ever committed to celluloid. Writers on the cinema have frequently observed that he was born to play Long John, but this might never have happened without the restrictions introduced during Sir Stafford Cripps' skinflint Chancellorship, which included the freezing of income owed to American film companies. Among those denied collection was Walt Disney, and, since the money could only be used in Britain, he considered starting a cartoon studio in London, then settled on the simpler expedient of shooting a live-action feature – his first venture in this genre. The result was a movie classic that would otherwise not have been made. Something else worth remembering is that, born to the part or not, Robert Newton has had formidable competition from rival Long Johns: Oscar-winning Wallace Beery in 1934 and the legendary Orson Welles in 1972. To have eclipsed men of this calibre is an astonishing achievement.

He gave further memorable performances in *Tom Brown's Schooldays* (1951), *The Desert Rats* (1953), *The High and the Mighty* (1954) and his last picture, *Around the World in 80 Days* (1956). *Treasure Island* also led to tailor-made vehicles like *Blackbeard, the Pirate* (1953), *Long John Silver* (1955) and an Australian TV series that again featured the peg-legged villain.

Robert Newton was six feet tall and, with striking dark good looks, swept many women off their feet and four of them up the aisle. Another enthusiasm was the sort of merrymaking that sometimes ended at 5.00 a.m. in a jail cell, where the constabulary would be regaled with stentorian Shakespeare soliloquies and side-splitting

This illustration from The Pirates Own Book *by Charles Ellms, published in 1837, may have influenced Robert Louis Stevenson in the creation of Long John Silver.*

Long John slapstick. The little time left over from these pursuits was principally devoted to the mismanagement of his affairs, resulting in bankruptcy to the tune of £45,000 in 1954 and, at the time of his death, two Hollywood lawsuits that could have cost him $600,000. He had a reputation for being difficult to work with; he was a man of intuition and inspiration, and once his interest in a part began flagging, producers held their breath and waited to see how impossible he might become. And yet he remained in constant demand.

He died in Hollywood of a heart attack on March 25th 1956 at the age of 50. His legacy, in financial terms, was less than he would have liked. But, as an artist, he left us real riches, above all his imperishable eye-rolling, lip-smacking, scenery-chewing Long John Silver.

Drink and the devil had done for the rest –
Yo-ho-ho, and a bottle of rum!

Bibliogaphy

Baring-Gould, Sabine. *Cornish Characters and Strange Events* (London, 1908)
Devonshire Characters and Strange Events (London, 1908)

Bevan, Bryan. *The Great Seamen of Elizabeth I* (London, 1971)

Botting, Douglas. *The Pirates* (London, 1978)

Burns, Sir Alan. *History of the British West Indies* (London, 1954)

Chatterton, E. Keble. *The Romance of Piracy* (London, 1914)

Course, A.G. *Pirates of the Eastern Seas* (London, 1966)
Pirates of the Western Seas (London, 1969)

Craton, Michael. *A History of the Bahamas* (London, 1962)

Dampier, William. *A New Voyage Round the World* (London, 1697)
Voyages and Descriptions (London, 1699)
A Voyage to New Holland (London, 1703, 09)

Defoe, Daniel. *A General History of the Robberies and Murders of the Most Notorious Pyrates* (London, 1724)
The King of Pirates (London, 1720)

Dunn, Richard S. *Sugar and Slaves* (London, 1973)

Ewen, C. L'Estrange. *The Pirates of Purbeck,* Proceedings of the Dorset Natural History and Archaeological Society, Volume 71 (Dorchester, 1949)

Firth, C.H. *Naval Songs and Ballads* (London, 1908)

Foss, Michael. *Undreamed Shores* (London, 1974)

Gosse, Philip. *The History of Piracy* (London, 1932)
The Pirate's Who's Who (London, 1924)

Grey, Charles. *Pirates of the Eastern Seas* (London, 1933)

Innes, Brian. *The Book of Pirates* (London, 1966)

Izon, John. *Sir Thomas Stucley* (London, 1956)

Johnson, W. Branch. *Wolves of the Channel* (London, 1931)

Langham, A. and M. *Lundy* (Newton Abbot, 1970)

Lloyd, Christopher. *The Brethren of the Coast* (London. 1960)
William Dampier (London, 1966)

Lloyd, Rachel. *Dorset Elizabethans* (London, 1967)

Maclay, Edgar S. *A History of American Privateers* (New York, 1899)

Masefield, John. *On the Spanish Main* (London, 1906)

Mitchell, David. *Pirates* (London, 1976)

Norman, C.B. *The Corsairs of France* (London, 1887)

Paine, Ralph D. *Joshua Barney* (New York, 1924)

Pringle, Patrick. *Jolly Roger* (London, 1953)

Ritchie, Robert C. *Captain Kidd and the War against the Pirates* (Cambridge, Mass., 1986)

Rogers, Woodes. *A Cruising Voyage Round the World* (London, 1712)

Rowse, A.L. *Sir Richard Grenville* (London, 1937)

Russell, Lord. *The French Corsairs* (London, 1970)

Senior, Clive. *A Nation of Pirates* (Newton Abbot, 1976)

Shipman, Joseph C. *William Dampier* (Lawrence, Kansas, 1962)

Snow, Edward Rowe. *Pirates and Buccaneers of the Atlantic Coast* (Boston, 1944)

Statham, E.P. *Privateers and Privateering* (London, 1910)

Wafer, Lionel. *A New Voyage and Description of the Isthmus of America* (London, 1699)

Wilkinson, Clennell. *William Dampier* (London, 1929)

Winston, Alexander. *No Man Knows My Grave: Privateers and Pirates 1655-1715* (Boston, 1969)